Assessing Your FITNESS

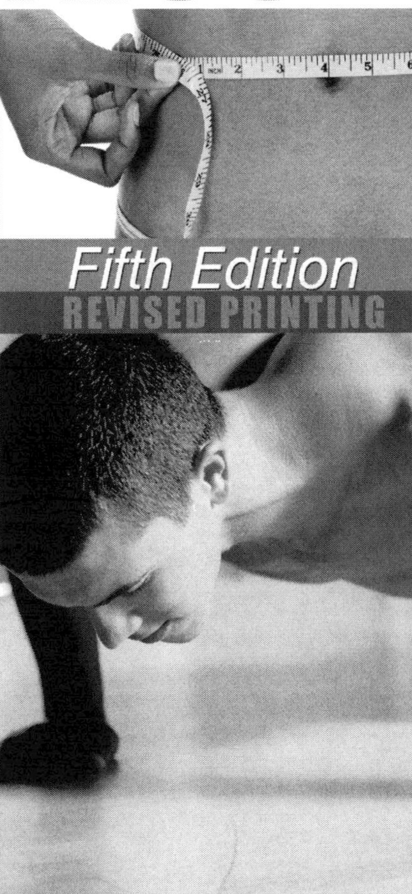

Fifth Edition
REVISED PRINTING

Jan Duquette
Duane Cain
Sommer McCartney

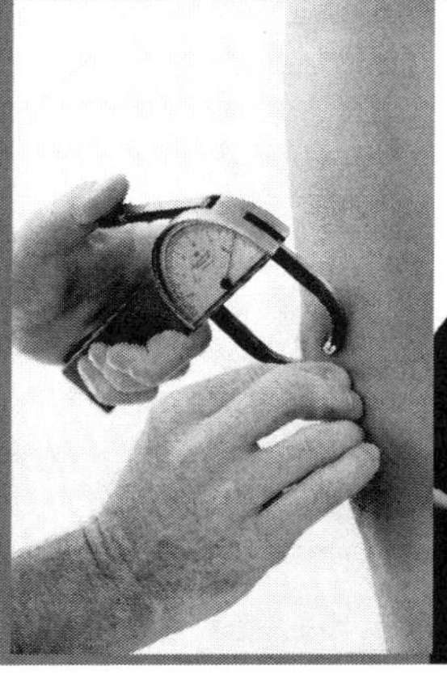

Kendall Hunt
publishing company

Formally published as Fitness Assessment Workbook

Cover image © JupiterImages, Inc. and Getty Images
All photos and images courtesy of the authors unless otherwise sourced.

Kendall Hunt
publishing company

www.kendallhunt.com
Send all inquiries to:
4050 Westmark Drive
Dubuque, IA 52004-1840

ISBN 978-1-7924-0129-9

Published in the United States of America

Dedication

To my niece, Rachelle, whose loving spirit keeps my life in perspective. . . . my family and friends whose love and support bring sunshine to all my days, and to those students whom I have taught over the years, and are a constant reminder that it is never too late to have fun achieving fitness—for a happier, healthier life.

Jan Duquette

This book is dedicated to my wife, Marion, who is my constant motivation and inspiration, also to the thousands of students throughout the years, whose dedication and efforts to improve their lifestyles have kept me going.

Duane Cain

To my wife, Kris, my mother, Jeanette, and the coaches and teachers that inspired me to go into this profession. Teaching enables me to educate and motivate others to live a healthier lifestyle.

Sommer McCartney

Contents

Preface

This *fitness assessment* book was written for college undergraduates, who, like the general public, are probably undergoing a barrage of media information related to fitness. These range from the best shoe to use while exercising or signing up for a particular fitness facility that will bring you the results they say you want. Revolutionary, new pieces of equipment are being advertised as being easy to use and better than anything else yet created—all for you! It is important to realize that many of these sales techniques try to push the 'hot buttons' for people without regard to the appropriateness of that activity for that person. As the title of our book implies, an assessment of your own health and fitness will provide you with information and a starting point upon which you can determine your pathway to a healthier lifestyle, and future fitness goals.

Our informative journey begins with the examination of your family history and the possible implications on your health. Particular attention will be directed toward coronary risk factors, including those criteria that cannot be changed, i.e., sex, age, and heredity, as well as those that may be altered, i.e., cholesterol and fat in the diet, hypertension, cigarette smoking and the lack of physical activity.

Additional health related fitness topics include an assessment of the student's body composition, indicating the ratio of lean muscle mass when compared to the body fat percentage. Another aspect of this adipose tissue determination is the part on the body where this excess fat is located. Measuring the circumference of the waist and comparing that to the circumference of the hip (waist to hip ratio), may result in a student with a high ratio, which appears to be correlated to a higher incidence of health problems, i.e., coronary heart disease and stroke.

Cardiovascular fitness, also known as aerobic fitness or even cardiorespiratory, since it really is a measure of the efficiency of the oxygen delivery system when combined with the circulatory system. By comparing a given volume of work and a resultant heart rate, an indication of the efficiency of their aerobic fitness can be measured. By assessing the range of motion and degree of flexibility of various joints, it can give the student some insight on potential difficulties, particularly the hamstring/lower back connection.

If the student wishes to increase their lean muscle tissue when compared to their body fat, it is necessary that the relative strength of various muscle groups be quantified. Whether this is limited to strength alone or coupled with muscle endurance, a measurement indicating the muscle strength is needed with a one repetition maximum effort. Awareness of the importance of the different types of muscle fibers can certainly lend insight into possible performance parameters for the student.

Another area of consideration falls under the title of skill-related fitness. A common denominator throughout is in the form of coordination, whether hand-eye or foot-eye, or the ability to perform complex movements. Examples of these fitness skills would be agility, or the ability to change direction quickly without sacrificing performance. Balance is demonstrating the capacity of maintaining equilibrium whether in a static or motionless position, as well as dynamic or balance while moving. Another aspect would be in the form of power, which is simply taking the strength that the student possess' and applying force or speed to move quickly, as in a jump. Speed, usually coupled with reaction time and movement time, is the final fitness skill, but it is not used since our assessment is not a workout class, and therefore should not risk injury to a student with an all out repetitive sprinting attempt.

A person with basic nutrition knowledge has the foundation upon which a sound dietary plan can be developed and followed. Recognition of the myths and fallacies surrounding nutrition is important, and the realization that some of them are the basis of which many quick weight loss plans are used. Weight management involves both a plan for losing fat off the body, (an increasingly major problem for the American public), as well as a plan for maintaining a healthy lifestyle.

One of the contributing factors in the difficulty of gaining and keeping a healthy and fit way of life, is the incidence of stress in our lives. A large majority of our student population, while certainly no different from the average American, is undergoing a series of subtle occurrences that may not be recognized as stress, and probably not resolved. Students are obviously facing various stresses related to their educational life, and decision making processes. Becoming aware of various stress situations and possibly acquiring alternative techniques that can result in a positive resolution, is certainly a desired outcome.

A well informed and educated person, knowing that some of the coronary risk factors may lead to a shorter or unhealthy life, could lay the foundation for a positive change. After having undergone a series of assessment measurements in the categories described in the preceding paragraphs, the student would be aware of their strengths and weaknesses. By following the guidelines found in each chapter, the student could chart out a sound program for reducing the shortcomings in their fitness profile. It is important for the student to realize that any plan for self improvement needs to be reevaluated periodically, and the appropriate adjustments made. Goals may change due to health reasons, age, finances or simply to face new challenges and to avoid boredom. Once sound fundamentals are understood and incorporated into the present lifestyle, then many of the corrections will be minor. It is hoped that this text will be of further value in the future as a reference or springboard to continued investigations of Fitness Assessment.

Acknowledgments

A number of people gave generously of their time in the creation of this book. We are grateful for the models whose pictures appear throughout the chapters: Janee' McCowan, Britton Ridenour, Paola Salazar, Woody Waite, Char Millang, Nicole Reed, Brooke Naughton, Briana McCartney and Kristen McCartney.

The authors are particularly indebted to the photographer, Andrea Fahy, whose original black and white photos were developed with much time and skill effort. A special thank you for your expertise.

We also thank the Saddleback College Kinesiology Faculty for their contributions in specific areas of fitness to help make this book encompass all realms of developing a healthy lifestyle.

Fitness Appraisal

KEY TERMS

Atherosclerosis
Blood pressure
Cholesterol
Coronary Heart Disease
Diastolic blood pressure
Fitness
Health risk appraisal
High density lipoprotein
Hypertension
Lipid
Lipoprotein
Low density lipoprotein
Medical history
Primary risk factors
Secondary risk factors
Sedentary
Systolic blood pressure

Are you interested in improving your health and fitness? Do you like the way you look and feel? Are you aware of the implications of your present lifestyle on your health and longevity? "Couch potato"! Sound familiar? Is the term 'fitness' a foreign language? Are you interested in your overall health and fitness now because it is required for your degree? What does it take to bring about a change in your health and fitness?

Start by becoming knowledgeable of your present health status through the use of a medical history questionnaire. Seek the answers to the influence of your heredity (blood relatives), by participating in a simple blood test. This may provide some answers regarding the genetic impact on some cardiovascular related diseases. All of these screening devices will aid in your search for more information regarding your health/fitness level.

Coronary heart disease is not just limited to the United States but can be found in many of the technologically/automated countries of the world. Risk factors that contribute to this sad state of health may be identified and indeed separated into two distinct yet interrelated conditions. Primary and secondary risk factors simply identify the weight and severity of those aspects of heredity and lifestyle that can lead to the increased chance of coronary heart disease.

PRIMARY RISK FACTORS

Primary risk factors seem to have the most significant influence on whether coronary heart disease will develop. However, the **secondary** risk factors do cause concern when they are added to the total number of risk factors present thus increasing the chance of CHD.

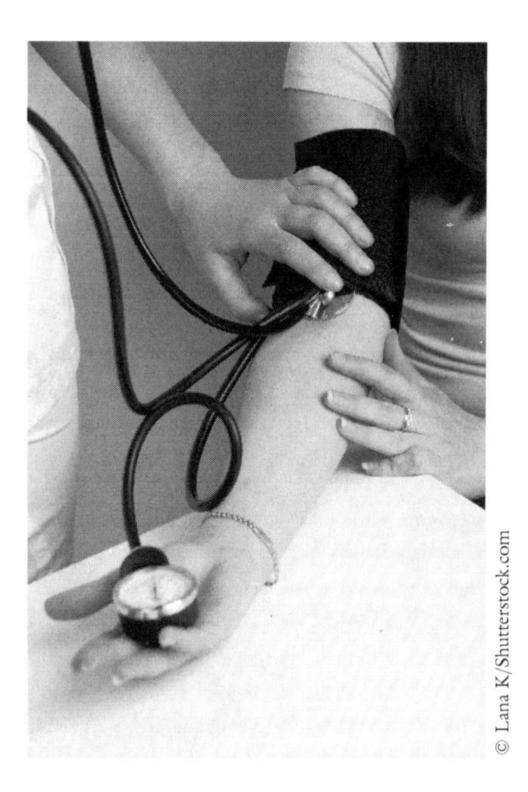

© Lana K/Shutterstock.com

Hypertension or high blood pressure, the 'silent killer', so called because of the lack of outward symptoms. It is usually a result of an ongoing elevation of blood pressure, either systolic (the pressure in the arterial walls during the work part of a heart beat or pulse) or diastolic (the pressure in the arterial walls on the resting phase between the heart beats), but quite often both. The readings from a blood pressure cuff that exceed 140 (systolic) over 90 (diastolic) would indicate a need for a recheck and to modify your lifestyle. Untreated hypertension could lead to CHD as well as an increased chance of a stroke.

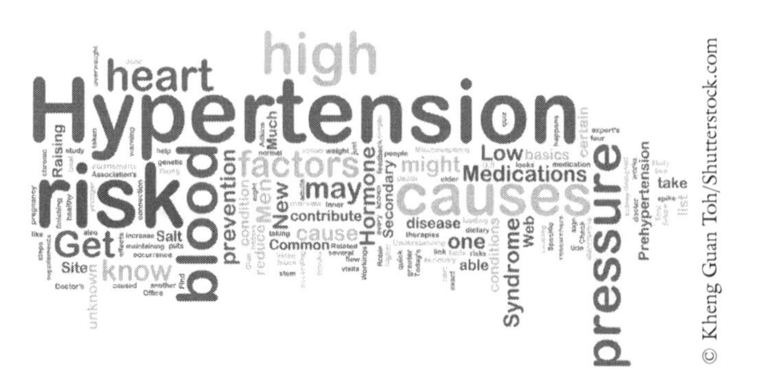

© Kheng Guan Toh/Shutterstock.com

Hyperlipidemia is an excess of the blood fats (lipids) that have accumulated in the arteries. These lipids may be in the form of cholesterol or serum triglycerides and are usually transported through the blood as a lipoprotein (a fat combined with a protein). This can be an inherited tendency, and by completing a fasting blood test, you would be aware of it and could take appropriate action.

	Desirable	Borderline	Undesirable
Cholesterol	200	200–239	240
LDL-C	<129	130–159	160
HDL-C	>40 Men >50 Women	35–44	35
TC/HDL Ratio	3.5:1	<5:1	>5:1

Table 1.1 Blood Cholesterol

Cholesterol is a fatty substance produced in the body, especially the liver, in addition to the very large amounts consumed in the typical diet. Cholesterol is not all bad, since it is essential in cell membrane composition and is used in the manufacture of bile (gall bladder) to help digest and absorb fats. It also assists in the formation of hormones that are responsible for male and female secondary sex characteristics. Excessively high total cholesterol (TC) amounts cause concern when the total reaches 240 mg/dl and above. (See Table 1.1.) TC is comprised of three lipoprotein components which are really descriptive of their size, large or VLDL, medium or LDL and small or HDL.

Very low density lipoproteins (VLDL) is a large molecule of fat with very little protein and correlates with the triglycerides risk. Usually not a very large number in the blood test panel.

Low density lipoproteins (LDL) is sometimes called the 'bad' cholesterol. Elevated levels of LDL (150+) have an affinity toward depositing the cholesterol into the arterial walls. This results in the narrowing of the available space, which is critical in the coronary arteries, thereby reducing the amount of blood capable of nourishing the heart.

High density lipoproteins (HDL) is also known as 'good' cholesterol. It appears that HDL-C is able to inhibit the deposit of the LDL plaque on the walls of the coronary arteries by transporting them to the liver for removal from the body. Therefore, the higher the amount of HDL-C in your blood indicates more resistance to the formation of atherosclerotic plaque. Regular exercise will elevate this protein factor in the cholesterol. As you will notice in Table 1.1, the best indicator of any potential CHD may be in the ratio of HDL-C to the total cholesterol (TC). A low ratio of 3 or 4:1, depending on age, would minimize the total amount of cholesterol as being the only concern and primary risk factor.

Cigarette Smoking. Of all the primary risk factors, smoking has a much higher influence on the possibility of developing CHD than any of the others. Most people are aware of the destructive relationship of smoking and lung cancer, but few realize that the chemicals and by products of cigarette smoke, including second hand smoke, significantly reduce the oxygen carrying capability of the blood feeding the heart muscle. The effectiveness of the HDL cholesterol appears to also be reduced by cigarette smoking. When a person stops smoking, that decision will drop their coronary risk factor very quickly.

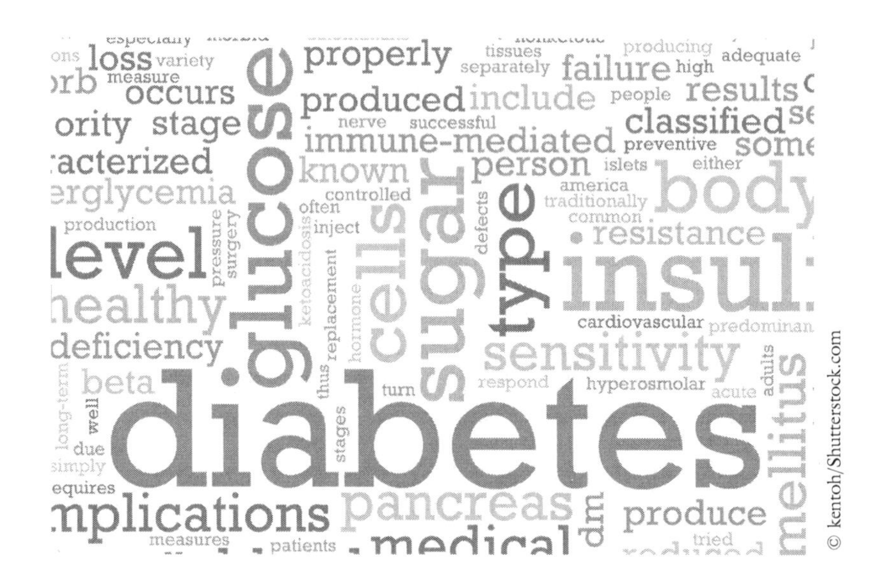

Diabetes Mellitus is characterized by a reduced or non-existent flow of insulin from the pancreas. The symptoms may vary depending on which type is present. Type I (15% of diabetics), also known as juvenile diabetes, and insulin dependent, is different than Type II (85%) adult onset diabetes, and is not insulin dependent. A Type I produces no insulin, is usually irreversible, while Type II does produce some insulin and can be usually traced back to some unhealthy lifestyle. Treatment similarities consist of diet, exercise, and stress management. Differences would be added insulin for Type I and possibly weight loss for Type II. A fasting blood test measuring glucose above 140 mg/dl would mean a possible need for a recheck since diabetes would be indicated.

Metabolic Syndrome is a combination of several disorders that affects 35% of adults and places them at higher risk of cardiovascular disease, diabetes, and stroke. Several primary cardiovascular risk factors along with insulin resistance characterize this syndrome. The American Heart Association and the National Heart, Lung, and Blood Institute recommend that Metabolic Syndrome be identified as the presence of three or more of the following components:

- Abdominal obesity
- Triglyceride level of 150 milligrams per deciliter of blood (mg/dL) or greater

- HDL cholesterol of less than 40 mg/dL in men or less than 50 mg/dL in women
- Systolic blood pressure (top number) of 130 millimeters of mercury (mm Hg) or greater
- Diastolic blood pressure (bottom number) of 85 mm Hg or greater
- Fasting glucose of 100 mg/dL or greater
- Insulin resistance or glucose intolerance (the body can't properly use insulin or blood sugar)

The keys to lowering your risk of metabolic syndrome are losing weight, increasing physical activity, eating a heart-healthy diet, monitoring blood glucose, cholesterol, and blood pressure.

Sedentary Lifestyle or low cardiovascular fitness puts additional stress on the heart muscle since it is not being strengthened and HDL-C receives little impetus for increasing. This also decreases the ability to reduce stress with some form of a physical outlet, i.e. regular exercise, which may also reduce some mild hypertension. Their susceptibility to overfatness and obesity, because of the overexposure to dietary fat, is compounded by their inactive lifestyle. There is even a term relating to a disease or condition reflecting a sedentary life and is called hypokinetic. 'Hypo' refers to too little or not enough and 'kinetic' means movement or energy expended. Diseases or conditions related to this pattern of inactivity would be heart disease, Type II diabetes, obesity and low back pain. Being busy does not qualify as an active lifestyle since there is usually little sustained expenditure of energy. Try walking, hiking, swimming, or biking for 30 minutes or more!

Family History. One of the primary risk factors that cannot be changed is the effect that heredity will play regarding potential coronary heart disease. If there is a history of blood relatives (parents, grandparents, brothers, sisters) having had any cardiovascular problems before the age of 50, then that genetic connection means an increased risk for the disease. It would be classified as a secondary risk if the age of the relative was older than 50.

SECONDARY RISK FACTORS

Secondary. Along with heredity there are some other unalterable factors that relate to the development of CHD.

Sex. Men have a higher incidence of developing heart disease than women, especially before the age of 45. Some researchers feel that the protection that women seem to enjoy may come from hormones that are in greater abundance during their pre-menopausal years. Some birth control pills may reduce the effectiveness of that protection.

Age. Men reaching 45 and women at 55 are both at increased risk. The difference in ages is the example of the role that hormones play in the womens' protection. Therefore, when a woman reaches menopause and the cessation of hormone production is completed, the risk of coronary heart disease is increased.

Obesity. Males with a body fat greater than 25%, and females more than 30% would be categorized as obese and have a weight problem. The influence of obesity is associated with hypertension, adult-onset diabetes, high cholesterol, atherosclerosis and an inordinate occurrence of cancers. This may be another relationship with hypokinetic disease, does their lack of active lifestyle occur as a result of obesity or the cause of it?

Triglycerides. This is another form of circulating fat in the blood, the majority arriving in fat we eat. Another concentration is found in the fat cells throughout the body where we store fat. Consumption of excess sugar and alcohol along with the fat will raise the triglycerides above the maximum desired level of 150 mg/dl. When the intake of triglyceride sources are reduced and controlled, and you embark on a good aerobics program, your risk for cardiovascular diseases will diminish.

Type A Personality/Stress. How a person reacts to any situation may depend on being identified as having type A or type B personality traits. Type A usually fall in the extreme of ambition, competition, time management, assertiveness and drive.

Type H Personality. There is a new personality linked to heart disease. The Type H personality refers to people with hostility and anger. It is the temper and distrust that makes you more susceptible to heart disease.

Uric Acid. This byproduct of protein metabolism is found in both the blood and urine. Elevated levels would be classed as a secondary risk for CHD. One symptom of a uric acid excess occurs with the inflammation of the large or second toes called gout.

Homocysteine is an amino acid that is found in our bloodstream and is produced by the body. Studies have shown that elevated levels of homocysteine are a risk factor to cardiovascular disease because it damages the inner lining (endothelial lining) of our arteries. This damage occurs due to the oxidation of LDL cholesterol. Plaque begins to adhere to the damaged site and therefore blocks the artery. Homocysteine levels can be reduced by increasing intake of folic acid (or folate), and vitamins B6 and B12. The FDA now requires the addition of folic acid in breads, cereals and grain foods.

It is important to realize that stress or worry over the factors that we have no control over may actually increase the incidence of health problems. Effort should be made toward changing the factors that you can control to make up for any deficiencies in the unalterable areas.

FIGURE 1.1 Fitness Wheel

CENTER FOR DISEASE CONTROL—MISSION STATEMENT: TO PROMOTE HEALTH AND QUALITY OF LIFE BY PREVENTING AND CONTROLLING DISEASE, INJURY, AND DISABILITY

Message from the Surgeon General 2010

Today's epidemic of overweight and obesity threatens the historic progress we have made in increasing Americans' quality and years of health life. Two-thirds of adults and nearly one in three children are overweight or obese. In addition, many racial and ethnic groups and geographic regions of the United States are disproportionately affected. The sobering impact of these numbers is reflected in the nation's concurrent epidemics of diabetes, heart disease, and other chronic diseases. (Message from the Surgeon General, 2010)

HEALTHY PEOPLE 2020 OBJECTIVES TOPIC AREAS

Healthy People provides research-based, 10-year national objectives for preventing disease and promoting health. Every 10 years, the U.S. Department of Health and Human Services (HHS) leverages scientific insights and lessons learned from the past decade, along with new knowledge of current data, trends, and innovations. Healthy People 2020 will reflect assessments of major risks to health and wellness, changing public health priorities, and emerging issues related to our nation's health preparedness and prevention.

Access to Health Services
Adolescent Health
Arthritis, Osteoporosis, Back Problems
Blood Disorders and Blood Safety
Cancer
Chronic Kidney Diseases
Diabetes
Disability & Secondary Conditions
Early and Middle Childhood
Educational & Community-Based Programs
Environmental Health
Family Planning
Food Safety
Genomics
Global Health
Health Communication & Health IT
Healthcare-Associated Infections
Hearing/Sensory or Communication Disorders
Heart Disease and Stroke
HIV
Immunization & Infectious Diseases
Injury & Violence Prevention
Maternal, Infant, & Child Health
Medical Product Safety
Mental Health & Mental Disorders
Nutrition and Weight Status
Occupational Safety & Health
Older Adults
Oral Health
Physical Activity & Fitness
Public Health Infrastructure
Quality of Life & Well-Being
Respiratory Diseases
Sexually Transmitted Diseases
Social Determinants of Health
Substance Abuse
Tobacco Use
Vision

Source: Office of Disease Prevention and Health Promotion. U.S. Dept. of Health and Human Services
(Full document available at: www.healthypeople.gov)

LIFE WITHOUT CIGARETTES
(American Cancer Society)
TIPS FOR ACTION (1-800-QUIT-NOW)

TO HELP CURB THE CRAVING: The following are different ways smokers can retrain themselves to live without cigarettes. Any one of several of these methods in combination might be helpful to you.

- Don't smoke after you get a craving for a cigarette until 3 minutes have passed. During those 3 minutes, change your thinking/activity.
- Don't store up cigarettes. Never buy a carton. Wait until one pack is finished before you buy another.
- Never carry cigarettes around with you at home or at work. Keep your cigarettes as far from you as possible. Leave them with someone or lock them up.
- Put away your ashtrays/fill them with objects so they can't be used.
- Change your brand of cigarettes weekly so you are always smoking a brand of lower tar and nicotine content than the week before.
- Always ask yourself, "Do I need this cigarette, or is it just a reflex?" Smoke only half a cigarette.
- Each day try to put off lighting your first cigarette.
- Decide arbitrarily that you will smoke only on even- or odd-numbered hours of the clock.
- Keep your hands occupied. Try playing a musical instrument, knitting, or fiddling with hand puzzles.
- Brush your teeth frequently to get rid of the tobacco taste/stains.
- If you have a sudden craving for a cigarette, take ten deep breaths, holding the last breath while you strike a match. Exhale slowly, blowing out the match, pretend the match was a cigarette by crushing it out in an ashtray. Now immediately get busy on some work.
- Get out of your old habits. Seek new activities or perform old activities in a new way. Don't rely on the old ways of solving problems. Do things differently.
- If you are a stay-home "kitchen smoker" in the morning, volunteer your services to schools or nonprofit organizations to get you out of the house. Take a shower . . . where you can't smoke.
- Stock up on light reading materials, crossword puzzles, and vacation brochures that you can read during your coffee breaks.
- Frequent places where you can't smoke, such as libraries, buses, theatres, swimming pools, department stores, or just go to bed.
- Give yourself time to think and get fit by walking a half hour each day. If you have a dog, take it for a walk with you.
- Don't skip meals (smokers often skip meals because they get an adrenaline rush from cigarettes that takes the place of eating).
- Eat less, more often. Snack on low-calorie vegetables and fruits.
- Drink six to eight glasses of water a day.
- Cut back on caffeine and alcohol, both are often associated with smoking.

(*Continued*)

LIFE WITHOUT CIGARETTES (American Cancer Society) TIPS FOR ACTION (1-800-QUIT-NOW) (*Continued*)

- Plan exercise into your daily routine. Run up stairs. Do some yardwork.
- Soak in the bathtub at the end of the day. This is a great relaxer.
- Don't use weight gain as an excuse to resume smoking. You must be 90 pounds overweight to rival the cardiovascular risk of smoking a pack of cigarettes a day.

HEALTHY PEOPLE 2020

Physical Activity and Fitness

Objectives Retained from 2010

1. Reduce the proportion of adults who engage in no leisure-time activities.
2. Increase the proportion of the nation's public and private schools that require daily physical education for all students.
3. Increase the proportion of adolescents who participate in daily school PE.
4. Increase the proportion of adolescents who spend at least 50% of school PE class time being physically active.
5. Increase the proportion of the nation's public and private schools that provide access to their physical activity spaces and facilities for all persons outside of normal school hours.
6. Increase the proportion of adults that meet current federal physical activity guidelines for aerobic physical activity and for muscle strength training.
7. Increase the proportion of adolescents that meet physical activity guidelines for aerobic physical activity and for muscle-strengthening activity.
8. Increase the proportion of children and adolescents that meet guidelines for television viewing and computer use.
9. Increase the proportion of employed adults who have access to and participate in employer-based exercise facilities and exercise programs.
10. Increase the proportion of trips made by walking and bicycling.

Objectives New for 2020

1. Increase the proportion of states and school districts that require regularly scheduled elementary school recess.
2. Increase the proportion of schools that require or recommend elementary school recess for an appropriate period of time.
3. Increase the proportion of physician office visits for chronic health diseases or conditions that include counseling or education related to exercise.
4. Increase the proportion of adults who perform physical activities that enhance or maintain flexibility.

Source: Office of Disease Prevention & Health Promotion. U.S. Department of Health and Human Services
(Full document available at: www.healthypeople.gov)

WORKSHEET 1

NAME ________________________________

Lifestyle Appraisal

NUTRITION AND WEIGHT MANAGEMENT

1. How many days a week do you eat a well-balanced diet that includes at least 2 servings from each of the following groups—Meat/meat substitutes, Dairy products, Fruit, Vegetables, Breads or Grains?
   ____________ (3) Frequently (5–6 Days)
   ____________ (1) Sometimes (3–4 Days)
   ____________ (0) Rarely (0–2 Days)
2. I eat food high in saturated fat, (Red meat, Fried foods, Butter/Margarine, Oils, Chocolate, Mayonnaise, Dressing).
   ____________ (0) Frequently (Just about every day)
   ____________ (1) Sometimes (Once about every day)
   ____________ (3) Rarely (Most days I don't eat any)
3. How often do you consciously limit both your salt and sodium intake?
   ____________ (3) Frequently (Almost everyday)
   ____________ (1) Sometimes (Every few days)
   ____________ (0) Rarely (Once a week or less)
4. I eat foods that are usually high in simple sugars which include Candies, Cookies, Cakes, Pastries, Ice Cream.
   ____________ (0) Frequently (At least once each day)
   ____________ (1) Sometimes (2–3 times a week)
   ____________ (3) Rarely (Hardly ever)
5. How often do you drink six 8 oz. glasses of water?
   ____________ (3) Frequently (Almost every day)
   ____________ (1) Sometimes (Every few days)
   ____________ (0) Rarely (Once a week or less)
6. How often do you eat at fast food restaurants?
   ____________ (0) Frequently (3 or more times a week)
   ____________ (1) Sometimes (Once or twice a week)
   ____________ (3) Rarely (Maybe once a month)
7. How often do you drink 8 oz. cups of caffeinated beverages? (Coffee, tea, soft drinks)
   ____________ (0) Frequently (6–10 times a day)
   ____________ (1) Sometimes (3–5 times a day)
   ____________ (3) Rarely (0–2 times a day)
8. I read the labels on foods to determine their nutritional values.
   ____________ (3) Frequently
   ____________ (1) Sometimes
   ____________ (0) Rarely
9. I am aware of the caloric content of foods I eat.
   ____________ (3) Frequently (I count calories)
   ____________ (1) Sometimes (I count only fat calories)
   ____________ (0) Rarely (I don't concern myself with calories)
10. I eat high fiber foods, (Whole Grains, Fresh Fruits, Vegetables) in my diet.
    ____________ (3) Frequently (2 or more times a day)
    ____________ (1) Sometimes (1–3 times a day)
    ____________ (0) Rarely (Hardly ever)

____________ SUBTOTAL

STRESS MANAGEMENT

1. I am able to express my feelings of anger or frustration to those around me.
   - ________ (3) Frequently
   - ________ (1) Sometimes
   - ________ (0) Rarely
2. When confronted with a crisis situation, I would be able to talk to my friends or family.
   - ________ (3) Frequently (Regardless of the topic)
   - ________ (1) Sometimes (Certain subjects)
   - ________ (0) Rarely (Communicating with them is impossible)
3. How often do you experience symptoms of excess stress such as tension, headaches, insomnia, diarrhea?
   - ________ (0) Frequently (3 or more times a week)
   - ________ (1) Sometimes (A few times a week)
   - ________ (3) Rarely (Less than once a week)
4. How often do you become irritable when you have to wait at a traffic light or any type of line, (at the market, bank, or amusement park)?
   - ________ (0) Frequently
   - ________ (1) Sometimes
   - ________ (3) Rarely
5. In response to stress and tension, how often do you use "quick fixes", i.e., alcohol, smoking, eating, or drugs, in an attempt to alleviate the situation?
   - ________ (0) Frequently (5 days a week)
   - ________ (1) Sometimes (A few days a week)
   - ________ (3) Rarely (Once a week or less)
6. How often do you worry about your work, school, or other deadlines during your free time?
   - ________ (0) Frequently (Just about every day)
   - ________ (1) Sometimes (Every couple of days)
   - ________ (3) Rarely (Once a week or less)
7. How often do you associate with people that have a positive attitude and make you laugh?
   - ________ (3) Frequently (Daily)
   - ________ (1) Sometimes (2–3 days a week)
   - ________ (0) Rarely (1 day a week or less)
8. How often do you come first, and are willing to say no to others?
   - ________ (3) Frequently (5 days a week)
   - ________ (1) Sometimes (Every couple of days)
   - ________ (0) Rarely (Never say no)
9. I am often able to accept feelings of sadness, anxiety, and depression, since they are only temporary.
   - ________ (3) Frequently
   - ________ (1) Sometimes
   - ________ (0) Rarely
10. I am often able to relax from my daily stress and tension.
    - ________ (3) Frequently
    - ________ (1) Sometimes
    - ________ (0) Rarely

________ **SUBTOTAL**

EXERCISE

1. How often do you exercise vigorously for a minimum of 20 minutes?
   ______________ (3) Frequently (4–6 days a week)
   ______________ (1) Sometimes (2–3 days a week)
   ______________ (0) Rarely (0–1 day a week)
2. How often do you exercise for muscle strength/endurance/toning (calisthenics or weight training)?
   ______________ (3) Frequently (4–6 days a week)
   ______________ (1) Sometimes (2–3 days a week)
   ______________ (0) Rarely (0–1 day a week)
3. How often do you participate in leisure-time activities (individual, with others or a team) that increase your level of fitness?
   ______________ (3) Frequently (3 or more hours)
   ______________ (1) Sometimes (1–2 hours)
   ______________ (0) Rarely (0 hours)
4. Compared to other people your own age and sex, how would you rate your present level of fitness?
   ______________ (3) Excellent
   ______________ (1) Fair
   ______________ (0) Poor
5. How often do you spend a minimum of 10 minutes a day stretching to increase your flexibility?
   ______________ (3) Frequently (4 or more days a week)
   ______________ (1) Sometimes (2–3 days a week)
   ______________ (0) Rarely (0–1 days a week)
6. How would you best describe your present body weight?
   ______________ (3) Happy with present weight (+ or − 5 pounds)
   ______________ (1) Like to change my weight (more than 10 pounds)
   ______________ (0) Like to change my weight (more than 20 pounds)
7. In an average week of housework, (vacuuming, laundry, cooking, cleaning), how many hours do you take?
   ______________ (3) 5 or more hours
   ______________ (1) 2–4 hours
   ______________ (0) An hour or less
8. In an average week, how many hours do you spend working in the garden or taking care of the yard?
   ______________ (3) Frequently (4 or more hours)
   ______________ (1) Sometimes (2–4 hours)
   ______________ (0) Rarely (An hour or less)
9. How many hours each day does your job require you to be on your feet and or moving around?
   ______________ (3) 5 or more hours
   ______________ (1) 2–4 hours
   ______________ (0) 1 hour or less
10. How often do you walk instead of drive, take stairs instead of elevators, or park at a distance to go shopping?
    ______________ (3) Frequently
    ______________ (1) Sometimes
    ______________ (0) Rarely

______________ **SUBTOTAL**

SCORING

Excellent	75–90	Total Points: ______________
Good	60–74	
Average	45–59	Rating: ______________
Below Average	15–44	
Poor	0–14	

CURRENT EXERCISE AND PHYSICAL ACTIVITY (MARK AN X ON DAYS YOU WORKOUT)

Activity	Sun.	Mon.	Tue.	Wed.	Thu.	Fri.	Sat.	Length of Workout
'Example' Walk		X		X			X	30 mins.

PHYSICAL EXERCISE

______________ I do not exercise on a weekly basis

______________ I exercise 2–3 days a week

______________ I exercise 4 or more days a week

______________ I am a competitive athlete in ______________

Glossary of Terms

Atherosclerosis is a very common form of arteriosclerosis, in which the arteries narrowed by the deposits of cholesterol and other material in the inner walls of the artery.

Blood pressure is the pressure exerted by the blood on the wall of the arteries.

Cholesterol is a steroid alcohol found in animal fats. This fat-like substance is implicated in the narrowing of the arteries in atherosclerosis.

Coronary heart disease (CHD) is atherosclerosis of the coronary arteries.

Diastolic blood pressure is the minimum blood pressure that occurs during the refilling of the heart.

Fitness is the state of well-being consisting of optimum levels of strength, flexibility, weight control, cardiovascular capacity and positive physical and mental health behaviors, that prepare a person to participate fully in life, to be free from controllable health-risk factors and to achieve physical objectives consistent with his/her potential.

Health risk appraisal is a procedure that gathers information about a person's behaviors, family history, and other characteristics known to be associated with the incidence of serious disease, and uses that information to compare the individual's present risks with the lower risks that could be achieved by changing certain behaviors.

High density lipoproteins is a type of lipoprotein that seems to provide protection against the buildup of atherosclerotic fat deposits in the arteries. Exercise seems to increase HDL.

Hypertension is persistent high blood pressure.

Lipid is a number of body substances that are fat or fat-like.

Lipoprotein is a combination of a lipid and protein. Cholesterol is transported in the blood plasma by lipoproteins.

Low density lipoprotein (LDL) is a lipoprotein carrying a high level of cholesterol, moderate levels of protein and low levels of triglycerides. Associated with the building of atherosclerotic deposits in the arteries.

Medical history is a list of a person's previous illnesses, present conditions, symptoms, medications and risk factors. Used to prescribe appropriate exercise programs. Persons whose responses indicate they may be in a high-risk category, should be referred for medical evaluation before beginning an exercise program.

Primary risk factors are risk factors that are strong enough to operate independently, without the presence of other risk factors.

Secondary risk factors are risk factors that acts when certain other risk factors are present.

Sedentary is sitting a lot; not involved in any physical activity that might produce significant fitness benefits.

Systolic blood pressure is blood pressure during the contraction of the heart muscle.

Related Websites

American Dietetic Association
www.eatright.org

American Heart Association
www.americanheart.org

Centers for Disease Control
www.cdc.gov

Go Ask Alice
www.columbia.edu/cu/healthwise

Healthfinder
www.healthfinder.gov
www.everydayhealth.com

Net Wellness
www.netwellness.com

Yahoo/Health
www.yahoo.com/health

Oncolink
www.oncolink.upenn.edu/

National Stroke Association
www.stroke.org

Smoking Cessation
www.quitsmoking.com

Study Questions

Name ______________________________

1. What are the various categories that represent the primary reasons that can result in coronary heart disease (CHD)?

2. What are the differences between systolic and diastolic blood pressure? Why is hypertension called the 'silent killer'?

3. How does the Surgeon General's Message 2010 describe the overall health of the U.S. population? How do *you* fit into the specifics of that report regarding obesity?

4. What steps can *you* take to diminish the effects of any primary and secondary risk factors?

5. Why does smoking cigarettes have such an influence on CHD?

6. What were 10 objectives for Healthy People 2020?

Cardiovascular Endurance and Flexibility

KEY TERMS

Aerobic	Flexibility	Oxygen debt
Anaerobic	Frequency	PNF stretch
Anaerobic threshold	Heart rate	Pulmonary
Artery	Heart Rate Reserve	Radial Pulse
ATP	Intensity	Rating of exertion
Ballistic movement	Interval training	Specificity
Cardiac output	Lactic acid	Steady state
Cardiovascular endurance	Ligament	Stroke volume
Carotid artery	Maximum heart rate	Submaximal
Cartilage	Maximal oxygen uptake	Target heart rate
Cool down	Muscle spindle	Tendon
Coronary arteries	Overload	Vein
Cross training	Overuse	VO_2 Max
Duration	Oxygen (O_2)	Warm up

Cardiorespiratory endurance, cardiovascular endurance, and aerobic fitness are synonymous terms. Cardiorespiratory refers to the health and function of the heart, lungs (pulmonary), and circulatory systems. Cardiovascular endurance refers to the heart, lungs, and blood vessels ability to deliver adequate oxygen to the exercising muscles. Cardio, as well as cardiac and coronary are all terms that refer to the heart. Blood which was pumped out of the ventricles of the heart, now travels to the lungs and gives up carbon dioxide and picks up oxygen from the air inhaled.

Generally, arteries carry blood with fresh oxygen supply away from the heart to capillaries, which are very small vessels where gases, nutrients, and cellular waste are exchanged between the blood and cells of the body. After passing through the capillaries, the blood, now lower in oxygen, enters the veins and flows back to the heart, which completes the cycle.

Cardiac output is the amount of blood pumped out of each ventricle each minute. Stroke volume is the volume of blood pumped out of the heart by the ventricles in one contraction.

The primary purpose of the cardiovascular system during exercise is to deliver oxygen and other nutrients to exercising muscle cells and carry carbon dioxide and other waste products away. When a muscle contracts and exerts force, the energy used to drive the contraction is a substance in the cell called ATP. ATP is the body's energy source. Muscle cells replenish ATP supply using different pathways. The Aerobic energy system metabolizes oxygen, and there is an adequate oxygen delivery into the cell to meet energy production. Anaerobic energy systems is without oxygen. In the absence of sufficient oxygen, i.e., when muscle cells needs to generate a lot of force very quickly, the cell shifts to anaerobic metabolism.

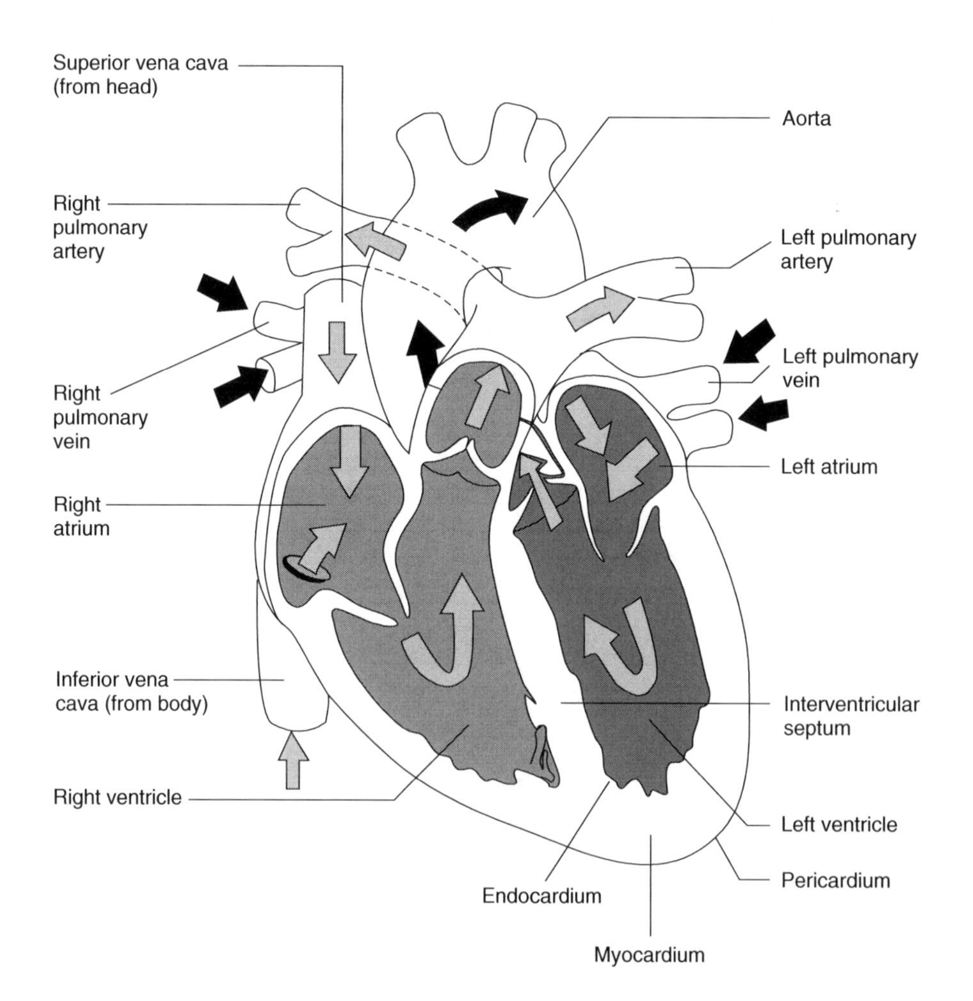

ENERGY SYSTEMS

Aerobic Energy

Aerobic energy system is submaximal exertion, requiring a constant supply of oxygen, available for use by the muscles. Aerobic work involves the large muscle groups, i.e., the legs at an intensity that can be sustained for a long period of time.

Anaerobic Energy

Anaerobic energy system provides a high rate of energy for short, intense, bursts of activity, usually not more than two minutes. Lactic acid is produced during this process and this contributes to muscle fatigue. These activities demand greater energy and oxygen than the capacity of the heart and circulatory system are able to produce.

MEASURING HEART RATES

Resting heart rate is more accurately measured in the morning just before getting out of bed. It can be taken for a full minute, or for 30 seconds and multiplied by 2 to find beats per minute.

Resting pulse can be measured on the radial artery on the wrist in line with the thumb. (Figure 2.1) Place the index finger and middle fingers over the artery and apply light pressure.

Exercise pulse is most accurately measured at the carotid artery, just to the side of the throat. (Figure 2.2) Heavy pressure should not be applied, as the pulse rate may slow. The exercise pulse should be taken for 6 seconds and multiplied by 10; or for 10 seconds and multiplied by 6 to find the beats per minute (BPM). Count the first pulse beat as 0 at the start of the 10 second count. Normal resting heart rate may range from 40–100 BPM, but an average resting heart rate for men is 70 BPM, and females 75 BPM. Endurance athletes usually have a lower resting heart rate due to an increased amount of blood pumped by the heart with each beat which equals stroke volume.

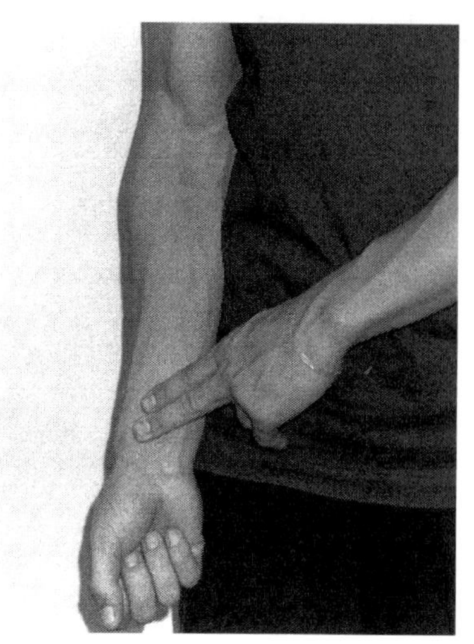

Figure 2.1 Radial pulse is taken with two fingers on the wrist at the base of the thumb

Figure 2.2 Carotid pulse is taken with 2 finger tips on the neck, just to the side of the throat

RESTING HEART RATES FEMALES

Beats Per Minute—Age in Years

Fitness Category	Under 30	30–39	40–49	50–59	60+
Superior	<47	<47	<47	<47	<47
Excellent	47–59	47–59	47–60	47–60	47–57
Good	60–64	60–65	61–65	61–65	58–64
Moderate	65–70	66–72	66–72	66–71	65–71
High	71–79	73–80	73–80	72–79	72–78
Very High	>80	>81	>81	>80	>79

RESTING HEART RATES MALES

Beats Per Minute—Age in Years

Fitness Category	Under 30	30–39	40–49	50–59	60+
Superior	<39	<39	<42	<42	<46
Excellent	39–54	39–55	42–54	42–55	47–55
Good	55–61	56–62	55–61	56–62	56–61
Moderate	62–68	63–67	62–67	63–67	62–67
High	69–79	68–79	68–82	68–82	68–82
Very High	>80	>80	>83	>83	>83

RATINGS OF PERCEIVED EXERTION (BORG SCALE)

This scale was created by Dr. Gunnar Borg. It takes into account perceptions of how someone feels while exercising, including exercise fatigue, environmental factors, psychological and physiological factors. This scale corresponds closely to someone's heart rate. An RPE of 15 would approximate a heart rate of 150.

Cardiovascular endurance is best measured either by direct measurement of oxygen consumption during maximum graded exercise testing (treadmill), or indirectly by estimating oxygen consumption from heart rate response to programmed increases in sub-maximal workloads (step test or 12 minute walk-run). Direct measurement of maximal oxygen consumption is the most accurate method, but requires special equipment and requires a maximum aerobic challenge. (Since you're going all out, a Doctor's presence is required). Basically, the more oxygen the body is able to use, the more work you are able to perform, before fatigue sets in.

Predicted Target Heart Rate Formula

The target heart rate (aerobic training zone) is 50–70% of your maximum. This is the target heart rate range recommended for maximum development of cardiovascular endurance.

		Example:	You:
Estimate of Maximum Heart Rate	220	220	220 BPM
	– Age	– 54	–( ) AGE
	Max. HR	166	( ) BPM
To find your target heart rate training zone:			
Max. Heart Rate is then multiplied	× .50	83	( ) BPM
Max. Heart Rate is then multiplied	× .70	116	( ) BPM

This 54 year old would then exercise in a target heart rate zone between 83–116 BPM. A 10-second count would be: 8–12.

Resting metabolic rate can also be estimated via equations such as the **Harris-Benedict formula.** Keep in mind that this formula carries with it a margin of error of +/– 10% and will estimate only the number of calories needed if you are completely sedentary. The use of this formula also assumes that you have a normal metabolic rate. If you have lost and regained large amounts of weight several times, you have likely permanently lowered your resting metabolic rate. Thus, the formula becomes somewhat-inaccurate.

Harris-Benedict Formula for Males:
66 + (6.22 × weight) + (12.7 × height in inches) – (6.8 × age) = daily calories necessary to support resting metabolism.

Harris-Benedict Formula for Females:
665 + (4.36 × weight) + (4.57 × height in inches) – (4.7 × age) = daily calories necessary to support resting metabolism.

After calculating the Harris-Benedict formula, multiply by the corresponding daily physical factor. Keep in mind that most people tend to overestimate their activity level. The calculated value gives an estimate of the number of calories one should consume daily to maintain current body weight.

Physical Activity Factor

1.1–1.2 Very light daily activity (standing, driving, sitting)
1.3–1.4 Light
1.5–1.6 Moderate
1.7–2.0 Heavy
2.1–2.4 Exceptionally heavy daily activity (competitive athlete)

The American College of Sports Medicine guidelines recommend that anyone over 35 years of age having one or more major risk factor and *everyone* over 45 years of age should undergo a physician supervised maximum graded exercise test before any other test or training takes place.

F.I.T. FORMULA FOR FITNESS	
F =	FREQUENCY (HOW OFTEN) Refers to the number of exercise workouts per week
I =	INTENSITY (HOW HARD) Refers to the speed or workload/resistance of exercise
T =	TIME (HOW LONG) Refers to the number of minutes of exercise at one time

F.I.T. FORMULA FOR CARDIOVASCULAR FITNESS

BEGINNER	INTERMEDIATE	ADVANCED
F = 3 to 5 Days Per Week	F = 3 to 5 Days	F = 4 to 7 Days
I = 40–60% Maximum Heart Rate	I = 50–70% Max.	I = 70–85% Max.
T = 10–20 Minutes Per Session	T = 20–45 Min.	T = 45–60 Min.

Cardiovascular workouts should alternate days preferably and also types of impact. If working out 5 days a week, individuals may choose to do impact activities, such as jogging or rope jumping on even days, and do non-impact activities, such as bike riding or swimming on odd days.

REASONS TO IMPROVE CARDIOVASCULAR FITNESS

DECREASES . . .	INCREASES . . .
Blood pressure	Heart volume
Resting heart rate	Resting & max. stroke volume
Total cholesterol	Maximum cardiac output
Body fat stores	Maximum oxygen consumption
Symptoms of depression, anxiety and tension	Capillary density and blood flow to active muscles
Glucose-stimulated insulin secretion	Heart function
Possible reduction in mortality in post myocardial infarction patients	HDL-cholesterol
	Aerobic work capacity
	Maximum ventilation
	Lung diffusion capacity
	Mobilization & utilization of fat

EXERCISE INTENSITY

Target heart rate for **moderate-intensity** 50% - 70%	Target heart rate for **vigorous-intensity** 70% - 85%
Activities of moderate intensity such as:	Activities of vigorous intensity such as:
Walking briskly (3 mph or faster)	Race walking, jogging, or running
Water aerobics	Swimming laps or jumping rope
Bicycling slower than 10 mph	Tennis (singles) or aerobic dancing
Tennis (doubles)	Heavy gardening (digging/hoeing)
Ballroom dancing	Bicycling 10 mph or faster
General gardening	Hiking uphill or with heavy backpack

GENERAL PRINCIPLES OF TRAINING

Overload: Subjecting the body to efforts greater than it is accustomed to elicit a training response; Increase the intensity or increase the time (duration).

Progression: A gradual increase in the frequency, intensity, and/or time, (duration) as fitness components improve.

Specificity: The principle that the body adapts very specifically to differential training stimuli. If you want to increase your flexibility, you may want to take a course in yoga.

Said: Specific Adaptation to Imposed Demand (workload). You can vary the workload in terms of:

Resistance	(tension)
Repetitions	(frequency of applying resistance)

TWO TYPES OF POPULAR TRAINING

Interval training is an increasingly popular type of training with the general public. Although it has been used by athletes for many years, it is being applied more with fitness enthusiasts. Two types of interval training are: 1) performance interval training—which is a very high intensity effort to enhance competitive performance for a specific sport, and 2) fitness interval training—a moderate to high intensity effort to improve general fitness. Fitness interval training programs are not as rigid and the increase in intensity is stopped when the anaerobic threshold is reached.

The basic principle of **cross training** is to rotate several fitness activities either on different exercise days or during one exercise session. This will help to alleviate overuse injuries, like tendinitis, and the stress of exercise will be on different areas.

Most people that are recreational exercisers need a variety of fitness activities, and by engaging in different workouts, the chance of becoming bored will be less and the calories burned will be higher.

FITNESS INTERVAL TRAINING

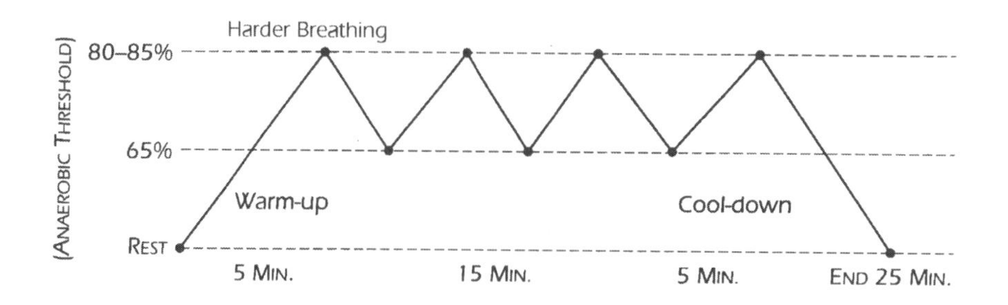

BASIC RULES FOR CROSS TRAINING

1. Alternate high-impact with low-impact activities.
2. Alternate energy-system activities (aerobics & anaerobics)
3. Every 3 months, take 1 week to do a different workout/sport.
4. If doing a new activity, start slow and do less.
5. At every third workout with the same class or exercise machine, change the intensity or difficulty of the workout.

FLEXIBILITY

Flexibility is a joint's ability to move freely in every direction, or more specifically, through a full range of motion (ROM) appropriate for that joint. Fitness professionals believe that flexibility is one of the most important components of physical fitness. Improving this component may mean achieving greater potential in your sport or activity. Stretching before and after an activity reduces the tearing of muscle tissue; increases the power of movement for the activity; increases metabolism in muscles, joint and associated connective tissues.

A number of factors can limit joint mobility, including genetic inheritance; the joint structure itself; connective tissue elasticity within the muscles, tendons, or skin surrounding the joint, and neuromuscular coordination. Flexibility training helps minimize the factors limiting range of motion.

Two types of flexibility are static and dynamic flexibility. **Static flexibility** is the ROM about a joint, with little emphasis on speed of movement. **Dynamic flexibility** is resistance to motion at the joint and involves speed during physical performance.

Most experts agree that a static stretch is the safest and most effective means of obtaining flexibility. One principle mentioned earlier in this chapter which is used for developing greater flexibility is the SAID principle. Specific Adaptation to Imposed Demands. The body, or connective tissue has the ability to adapt to the stresses placed upon it during physical activity. However, if it is overstretched, stretched too vigorously or for an excessive length of time, it will weaken structurally, leading to serious injury.

BENEFITS OF FLEXIBILITY

© SHISHOV MIKHAIL/Shutterstock.com

1. Increased physical efficiency and performance.
2. Decreased risk of injury.
3. Increased blood supply and nutrients to joint structures.
4. Increased quality and quantity of joint synovial fluid.
5. Increased neuromuscular coordination.
6. Reduced muscular soreness.
7. Improved muscular balance and postural awareness.
8. Decreased risk of low-back pain.
9. Reduced stress.
10. Enhanced enjoyment.

THREE BASIC TECHNIQUES FOR INCREASED FLEXIBILITY

PNF—Proprioceptive Neuromuscular Facilitation

Based on Herman Kabat's therapeutic principles, this hold-relax method of stretching promotes improved performance through greater range of motion and enhancement of amplitude of each movement, greater muscle relaxation, and fewer injuries to muscle and connective tissue. Hold-relax incorporates the muscle being contracted "held" for five seconds against a resistance. Then as it is "relaxed" for five seconds, the opposing or antagonistic muscles will move it gently into a new broader range of motion.

The PNF with partner hamstring stretch is done with one person laying down on their back with both legs extended on the floor. The leg to be stretched is brought up in the air to a point of tightness in the back of the leg, (when you feel the muscles meeting resistance). The leg remaining on the floor is kept straight to enhance stretching. The partner will kneel and place his shoulder under the heel of the raised leg, (he serves as an immovable object.) The person being stretched will push his leg against the shoulder of the kneeling partner. The hold phase begins when the person being stretched attempts to push his leg back toward the floor against the partner's shoulder.

Static Stretching

This involves a slow, gradual, and controlled stretch through a full range of motion. A person stretching his calf muscle would stand and lean over (with back straight) the forward knee until feeling a pull (without pain) in the calf and hold the position for 15–30 seconds. Less injuries to the tissues result with this low-intensity, long-duration technique, and there will be greater flexibility gains. The **stretch reflex** is suppressed by stretching done in this manner. Another reason that this technique is so popular, is it diminishes the chances of getting delayed muscle soreness. (This sometimes occurs 24–48 hours after strenuous exercise).

Dynamic Stretching

Dynamic stretching or ballistic stretching, consists of quick, repetitive bouncing type movements. Uncontrolled or excessive movements can also easily overload soft tissue structures beyond normal elastic capabilities. This type of stretch can result in damage to muscle and connective tissue, and may be responsible for increased muscle soreness. Most fitness experts feel ballistic stretching is the *least* beneficial stretching technique and is also often unsafe.

GENERAL RULES FOR STRETCHING SAFELY

1. Avoid hyperextension of the spine. (Back or forward)
2. Avoid locking any joint. (Keep joints soft or slightly bent)
3. Never force a movement. (Keep the body in natural positions)
4. Avoid forward flexion of the spine. (Compresses low back)

WARMING UP FOR A SAFE WORKOUT

Warming-up and stretching are actually two different terms. The body should first be "warmed-up" by doing a circulatory workout. This will increase the body temperature, blood saturation, allow the heart to adjust to the increased demand, and the metabolic reactions that produce fuel for activity will occur more quickly and efficiently. Performing 4–6 minutes of warm-up should be sufficient, however, the colder the environment the longer the circulatory warm-up . . . 10–15 minutes. Examples include: Walking with arm movements; Slow cycling, swimming or jogging; Mild rope jumping; Low-intensity aerobic or step routine.

Stretching warm-up then follows the circulatory warm-up, and involves 3–5 minutes of mild stretches. The purpose is to prepare your body for the stress of exercise. *Stretch first to prevent injury, stretch last to increase or maintain flexibility.*

The final stretch is done after you have completed your cardiovascular or muscular workout. This stretch serves as a final cool-down. You should feel slightly fatigued, but not exhausted. Your temperature and heart rate should be close to your resting levels, and the perspiration should be nearly evaporated.

THE FIVE MINUTE STRETCH

Hold 10 Sec. Ea & Relax

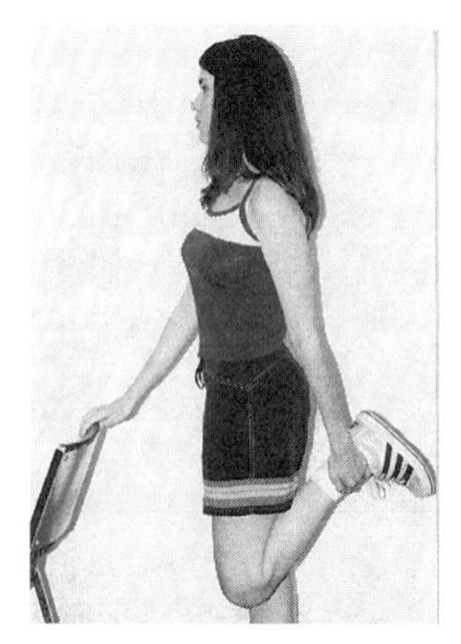

1. Standing Quad Stretch w/ Chair

2. Standing Rear Calf Stretch

3. Alternating Forward Arm Raises

4. Rear Arm Stretch Behind Back

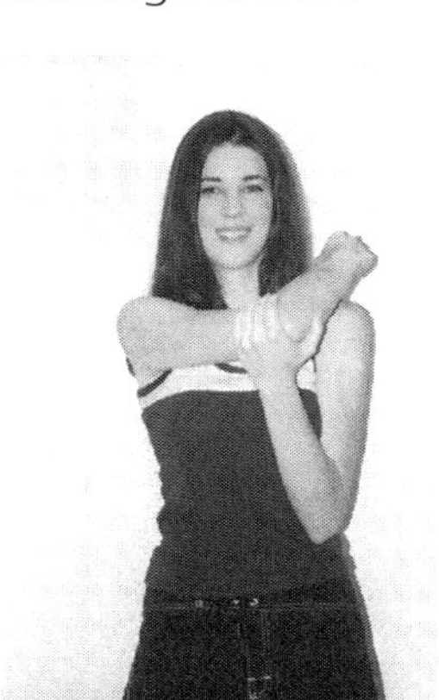

5. Alternating Arms Across Chest

6. Head Tilts R/L & Head Turns R/L

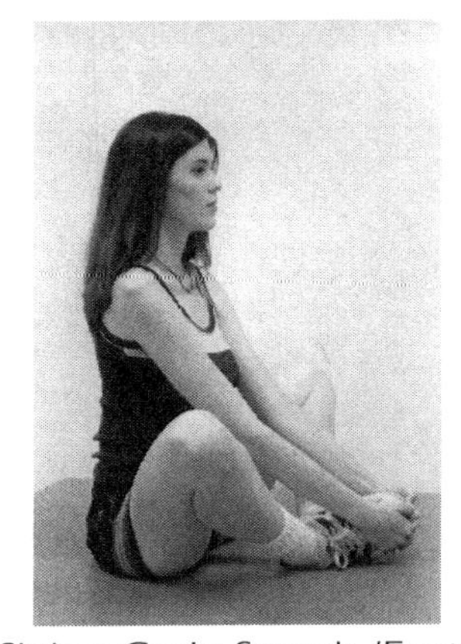

7. Sitting Groin Stretch (Feet In)

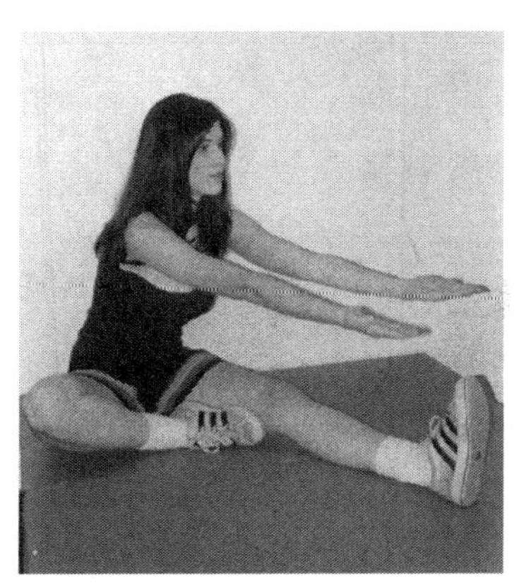

8. Modified Hurdler's Stretch (In)

9. Hamstring Stretch on Back (L/R)

10. Knees to Chest for Low Back

CONTRAINDICATED STRETCHING EXERCISES
(Do's and Don'ts of Flexibility Stretches)

Low Back Stretch

FIGURE 2.3 DO—Stretch your low back with a double knee flex to the chest. On your back gently pull both knees toward chest, hold and relax. This may also be done with one leg. Hold legs beneath your knee caps

FIGURE 2.4 DON'T perform an unsupported forward flexion. This places excessive stress on the lumbar structures. The knees also hyperextend and the risks outweigh the benefits

Hurdler's Stretch

FIGURE 2.5 DO—Keep the knee soft, the spine straight, and go forward until you feel tension. Modified hurdler's stretch is much safer

FIGURE 2.6 DON't perform this with the knee bent backward. It overstretches ligaments and tendons on the bent knee

Hamstring Stretch

FIGURE 2.7 DO—Lie on back, with knees bent and feet flat on floor. Raise one leg without lifting hips. Grasp the leg below the knee to increase the stretch. This is the safest way to increase flexibility in the hamstrings

FIGURE 2.8 DON'T do this straight leg stretch unless you are flexible enough to keep your spine straight. Knees hyperextend & shoulders are rounded, which causes discomfort

LOW BACK HEALTH

Low back pain, injury and other back disorders may be the most pressing health problem in modern America, at least in terms of prevalence if not severity. Low back problems affect as many as 80% of all persons during their lifetime.

Causes associated with low back pain: Prolonged sitting, or a sedentary lifestyle; Improper sitting/posture in general; Visceral Ptosis/pot belly; Emotional stress/anxiety; Occupation (lifting and carrying loads); Aging (normal wear and tear with age); Muscular weakness and/or imbalance; Sports or previous injury; and Cigarette smoking (indirect, but more likely).

Muscular imbalances: Kyphosis—Hip displace backward, shoulders rounded, flattens lumbar. Lordosis—Hips displace forward, and excessive curvature of the low back. Scoliosis—A lateral curvature of the spine.

TIPS FOR PREVENTION

Exercising

Minimize forward flexion.

Avoid staying in positions for long periods of time.

Avoid rotation (twisting) and flexion together.

Avoid ballistic (bouncing) movements.

Breathe naturally.

Good technique and balance.

If it hurts . . . don't do it.

Practical

Shoes should be well cushioned, offer ample support, & have low heels.

Work surfaces should be at a comfortable height.

Chairs should have good lower back support.

If you sit for long periods, rest your feet on the floor, or a stool.

If you stand, rest one foot on a low stool.

When driving, cushion the small of your back with a pillow.

Stop occasionally, to stretch your back on long trips.

At Home

Try sleeping on your back with a pillow under your knees.

Try sleeping on your side with your knees bent.

Keep lifted items close to your body.

Don't lift while twisting, bending forward, or reaching.

Staying in shape is the most important thing you can do to prevent future lower back problems.

LOW BACK EXERCISES

Single Knee to Chest —Lie on back. Pull one knee up toward chest as far as you can. Hold 10–60 seconds. Then do opposite knee. Next, perform double knee to chest.

Double Knee to Chest —Now pull both knees toward chest. Hold 10–60 seconds. Alternate single knee in to chest, then both.

Pelvic Tilt —Lie on back with knee bent. Tighten abdominal muscles, squeeze buttock muscles and flatten back. Hold 10–60 Seconds.

Buttocks Raise —Lie on back, knees bent. Tighten buttocks and raise as high as you can. Keep pelvis level. Hold 10–60 seconds.

Advanced Buttocks Raise —Lie on back with leg bent. One leg is extended straight out. Tighten buttocks and raise them off the floor. Keep pelvis level. Hold 10–60 seconds.

Abdominal Crunch —Lie on back with knees bent. Place hands behind head. Without pulling with your hands, raise head and shoulders . . . curl trunk upward. Hold 10–60 seconds.

Abdominal Rotation —Lie on back with knees bent. Place hands behind head. Without pulling with your hands, raise head and shoulders. Curl trunk upward to the side, & hold 10–60 seconds.

Hamstring Stretch —Lie on back holding leg with hands. Keep opposite knee bent. Straighten the knee as far as you can. Hold 10–60 seconds.

Sitting Hamstring Stretch —Sit with leg propped up on a chair. Relax, letting the leg straighten, so that the stretch is felt. Hold 10–60 seconds. Repeat on the other leg.

Doorway Stretch —Lie on back with leg propped in doorway. Keep the opposite leg straight on the floor. Lie as close to the base of doorway as possible, while keeping legs straight. Hold 10–60 Sec.

Positional Hamstring Stretch —Sit on floor with low back against couch. Watch TV and allow to gently stretch low back & hamstrings. Stretch for as long as you can tolerate.

Lumbar Rotation —Lie on back with knees bent and feet together, arms out to the side. Rotate knees to each side—turn head to opposite side. Hold 10–60 seconds.

Lumbar Rotation—Progression —Lie on back with legs straight, arms out to side. Cross L knee over body, turning head opposite direction, until you feel a stretch. Hold 10–60 seconds. Then do R.

Cat-Cow —Assume hands and knees position. Tighten abdominal muscles, squeeze buttock muscles and tuck tailbone under, hunch back upward and then relax.

Back Stabilization —Assume hands and knees position. Keeping back level, raise one arm and opposite leg. Hold 10–60 seconds, repeat with opposite arm and a leg.

Back Extension —Assume front lying position. Prop yourself up using elbows as support, palms flat on the floor. Hold for 10–60 sec.

Back Extension—Progression —Assume front lying position, and place hands on floor under shoulders, as in a push-up starting position. Straighten arms to press trunk upward, letting hips sag toward floor. Hold 10–60 seconds.

Back Extension—Sitting Posture Break —Sit with back against chair. Reach upward and lean backward until you feel a stretch. Hold 10–60 seconds. This may be done throughout the day.

Scapular Pinch —Stand with arms at sides. Pinch shoulder blades together. Hold 10–60 seconds. Squeeze throughout the day as needed.

Side Bend —Clasp hands together and lean to each side until you feel a stretch. Hold 10–60 seconds.

Golf Rotation Stretch —Sit on a bench or stand holding golf club. (Club is placed behind the neck and arms are outstretched to horizontal with hands hanging forward over club). Rotate trunk to each side until you feel a stretch. Hold 10–60 seconds.

ALTERNATIVE LOW BACK TREATMENTS—DECIDE WHAT'S BEST FOR YOU

Analgesics —Over-the-counter pain relievers such as acetaminophen, aspirin, or other non-steroidal anti-inflammatory drugs, such as ibuprofen or naproxen, can usually relieve backache suffering. Codeine pain relievers can cause drowsiness and are addictive.

Heat and Cold Treatment —Cold packs are suggested for the first day or two after pain begins and heat thereafter.

Spinal Manipulation —Self-adjustment to the spine should only be done if properly trained, or by an osteopath or chiropractor. If you are not better in 4 weeks, see your primary-care clinician.

Physical Activity —Good muscle tone is *crucial* to recovery, and every day spent in bed results in the loss of 1% of muscle mass. If you are in bed, try to get up and walk every 2–3 hours. Then gradually try moderate exercise (stationary bicycle, swimming).

Other Therapies —The following are potentially expensive and unlikely to solve the problem: massage, traction, transcutaneous electrical nerve stimulation (TENS), biofeedback, acupuncture, ultrasound, and injection.

Figure 2.5 Static Stretching

F.I.T. FORMULA FOR FLEXIBILITY	
F =	3 Days a Week Minimum (Static or PNF Stretches)
I =	Just Below Pain Threshold (When You Feel the Muscles Tighten)
T =	10–12 Exercises (2–6 Repetitions) 10–60 Seconds of Stretch & Relax

WORKSHEET 2 NAME ____________________

Cardiovascular Endurance

List three aerobic activities. List three **different** fitness benefits you receive that are unique for each activity:

AEROBIC ACTIVITY #1	FITNESS BENEFITS
____________________	1.
	2.
	3.

AEROBIC ACTIVITY #2	FITNESS BENEFITS
____________________	1.
	2.
	3.

AEROBIC ACTIVITY #3	FITNESS BENEFITS
____________________	1.
	2.
	3.

(COMPLETE THE OTHER SIDE)

FLEXIBILITY

Lack of shoulder flexibility is second only to low back pain. Describe/illustrate 4 stretches that would increase range of motion of the **shoulder joint**: (Use your imagination or draw from past experience.)

1.

2.

3.

4.

LAB 1

Cardiovascular Fitness Test

THREE-MINUTE STEP TEST

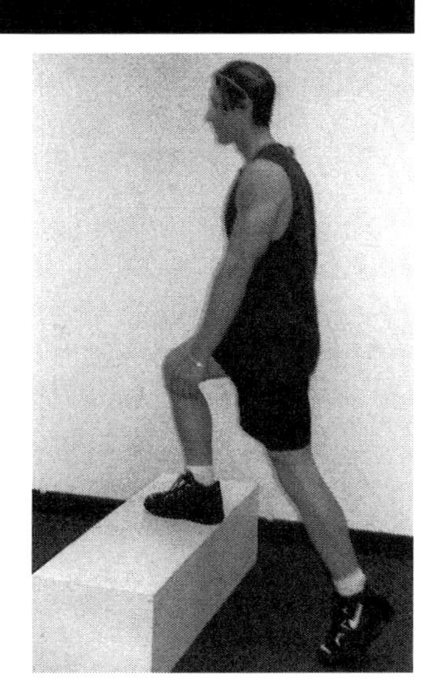

PURPOSE: The Step Test measures the heart rate in a 1-minute recovery period.

EQUIPMENT: 12″ Bench, Stopwatch, Cue tape

PROCEDURE: Each student steps up and down at 24 beats a minute, for three minutes. Immediately after the three minutes of stepping each student will sit down. A 60-second heart rate is taken, starting 5 seconds after the completion of stepping. If the student does not complete the test, it is an automatic Very Poor.

MEN (YEARS OF AGE)

Fitness Category	18–25	26–35	36–45	46–55	56–65	65+
Excellent	<79	<81	<83	<86	<87	<88
Good	79–99	81–99	83–103	86–103	87–105	88–103
Average	100–105	100–107	104–112	104–112	106–116	104–113
Below Average	106–128	108–128	113–130	113–129	117–132	114–130
Poor	>128	>128	>130	>129	>132	>130

WOMEN (YEARS OF AGE)

Fitness Category	18–25	26–35	36–45	46–55	56–65	65+
Excellent	<85	<88	<90	<90	<94	<95
Good	85–108	88–111	90–110	90–115	94–115	95–112
Average	109–117	112–119	111–118	116–122	116–120	113–118
Below Average	118–140	120–138	119–140	123–134	121–135	119–139
Poor	>140	>138	>140	>134	>135	>139

Source: Saddleback College

RECOVERY PULSE ______________ FITNESS CATEGORY ______________

LAB 1

12-Minute Walk/Run Test

CARDIOVASCULAR ENDURANCE

PURPOSE: A field test of aerobic capacity and oxygen consumption.

EQUIPMENT: 440-yard track or treadmill, whistle, watch.

PROCEDURE: Participants will walk/jog/run as far as possible in 12 minutes. Count the number of laps completed. When the whistle sounds, add the partial lap to your total. (Refer to diagram.)

DISTANCE COVERED:

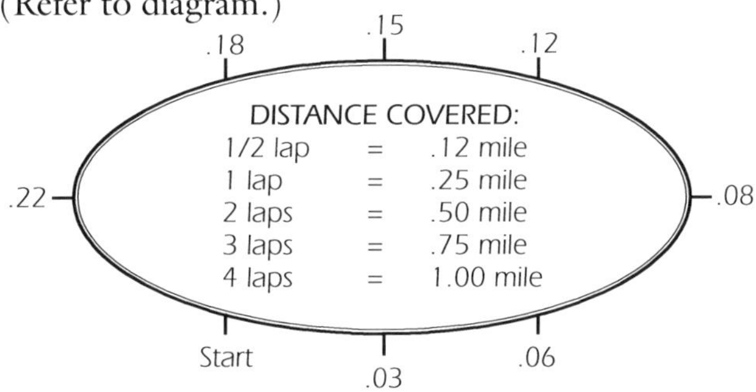

DISTANCE (MILES COVERED IN 12 MINUTES)

Years of Age

Fitness Category	<29	30–39	40–49	50–59	60+
Men					
Excellent	>1.73	<1.67	<1.61	<1.53	<1.41
Good	1.58–1.72	1.55–1.66	1.48–1.60	1.38–1.52	1.29–1.40
Average	1.49–1.57	1.45–1.54	1.38–1.48	1.29–1.37	1.19–1.28
Below Average	1.37–1.48	1.33–1.44	1.28–1.37	1.18–1.28	1.08–1.18
Poor	<1.36	<1.32	<1.27	<1.17	<1.07
Women					
Fitness Category	<29	30–39	40–49	50–59	60+
Excellent	>1.54	>1.45	>1.40	>1.29	>1.20
Good	1.41–1.53	1.39–1.44	1.29–1.39	1.11–1.28	1.09–1.19
Average	1.22–1.40	1.18–1.38	1.11–1.28	1.05–1.10	.98–1.08
Below Average	1.11–1.21	1.05–1.17	.98–1.10	.93–1.04	.86–.97
Poor	<1.10	<1.04	<.97	<.92	<.85

Source: Saddleback College

MILES COVERED ______________ FITNESS CATEGORY ______________

LAB 1

Flexibility Test

SIT AND REACH

(No general flexibility test measures the flexibility of all joints; however, the sit and reach test serves as an important measure of hip and back flexibility.)

PURPOSE: Due to widespread problems of low back pain and joint soreness, flexibility tests are necessary to determine the functional ability of the joints to move their full range of motion.

EQUIPMENT: Box or curb, and a yardstick on top with 15" mark at the edge.

PROCEDURE: Sit on the floor with legs straight, and feet 10–12" apart up against the box. Slowly reach forward with both hands, exhaling and extending your stretch as far as possible and hold for 3 seconds. Exhale on effort. Note the farthest point you can reach on the stick with your fingertips even. (Shoes removed.)

		Men			
Fitness Category	<29	30–39	40–49	50–59	60+
Excellent	20+	20+	18+	17+	17+
Good	17–19	17–19	16–17	15–16	14–16
Average	16–17	15–16	14–15	13–14	12–13
Below Average	14–15	13–14	12–13	10–12	10–11
Poor	<14	<13	<12	<10	<10
		Women			
Fitness Category	<29	30–39	40–49	50–59	60+
Excellent	22+	21+	20+	20+	19+
Good	20–21	20–19	18–19	18–19	17–18
Average	19	18	17	17	16
Below Average	17–18	16–17	15–16	15–16	13–15
Poor	<17	<16	<15	<15	<13

Source: ACSM (American College of Sports Medicine)

INCHES ______________ FITNESS CATEGORY ______________

Glossary of Terms

Aerobic means using oxygen.

Anaerobic means not using oxygen.

Anaerobic threshold is the point where increasing energy demands of exercise cannot be met by the use of oxygen, and an oxygen debt begins to be incurred.

Artery is a vessel which carries blood away from the heart to the tissues of the body.

ATP (adenosine triphosphate) is an energy-rich compound and when broken down provides energy used by all energy-required processes of the body.

Ballistic movement is an exercise movement in which a part of the body is "thrown" against the resistance of antagonist muscles or against the limits of a joint. The latter, especially, is considered dangerous to the integrity of ligaments and tendons.

Cardiac output is the volume of blood pumped out by the heart in a given unit of time. It equals the stroke volume times the heart rate.

Cardiovascular endurance pertains to the heart, blood vessels, and lungs ability to continue a physical performance over a period of time.

Carotid artery is the principle artery in both sides of neck. A convenient place to detect the pulse.

Cartilage is fibrous connective tissue between the surfaces of movable and immovable joints.

Cool down is a gradual reduction of the intensity of exercise to allow physiological processes to return to normal. Helps avoid blood pooling in the legs and may reduce muscle soreness.

Coronary arteries are the arteries, circling the heart like a crown, that supply blood to the heart muscle.

Cross training is the practice of alternating exercise choices throughout the week to avoid overuse injuries from repetitive movements.

Duration is the time spent in a single exercise session. Duration, along with frequency and intensity, are factors affecting the effectiveness of exercise.

Dyspnea is difficult or labored breathing.

Flexibility is the range of motion around a joint.

Frequency is how often a person repeats a complete exercise session (e.g. 3 times per week). Frequency, along with duration and intensity affect the effectiveness of exercise.

Heart rate is the number of beats per minute.

Heart rate reserve is the difference between the resting heart rate and the maximum heart rate.

Intensity is the rate of performing work power. A function of energy output per unit of time. Intensity, along with duration and frequency, affect the effectiveness of exercise.

Interval training is an exercise session in which the intensity and duration of exercise are consciously alternated between harder and easier work. Often used to improve aerobic capacity and/or anaerobic endurance in exercisers who already have a base of endurance training.

Lactic acid is the end product of the metabolism of glucose for the aerobic production of energy.

Ligament is the fibrous, connective tissue that connects bone to bone, or bone to cartilages, to hold together and support joints.

Maximum heart rate is the highest rate of which an individual is capable. A broad rule of thumb for estimating maximal heart rate is 220 (beats per minute) minus the person's age (in years).

Maximal oxygen uptake is the highest rate of oxygen consumption of which a person is capable. Usually expressed in milliliters of oxygen per kilogram of body weight per minute. Also called maximum aerobic power, maximal oxygen consumption, maximal oxygen intake.

Muscle spindle is the organ in a muscle that senses changes in muscle length, especially stretches. Rapid stretching of the muscle results in messages being sent to the nervous system to contract the muscle, thereby limiting the stretch.

Overload is subjecting a part of the body to efforts greater than it is accustomed to, in order to elicit a training response. Increases may be in intensity or duration.

Overuse is excessive repeated exertion or shock which results in injuries such as stress fractures of bones or inflammation of muscles and tendons.

Oxygen (O2) is the essential elements in the respiration process to sustain life. The colorless, odorless gas makes up about 20 percent of the air, by weight at sea level.

Oxygen debt is the oxygen required to restore the capacity for anaerobic work after an effort has used those reserves. Measure by the extra oxygen that is consumed during the recovery from work.

PNF (Proprioceptive Neuromuscular Facilitation) Stretch are muscle stretches that use the proprioceptors (muscle spindles) to send inhibiting (relaxing) messages to the muscle that is to be stretched.

Pulmonary is pertaining to the lungs.

Radial pulse is the pulse at the wrist.

Rating of Perceived Exertion is a means to quantify the subjective feeling of the intensity of an exercise. Borg scales, charts which describe a range of intensity from resting to maximal energy outputs, are used as a visual aid to exercisers in keeping their efforts in the effective training zone.

Specificity is the principle that the body adapts very specifically to the training stimuli it is required to deal with. The body will perform best at the specific speed, type of contraction, muscle-group usage and energy source usage it has become accustomed to in training.

Steady state is the physiological state, during submaximal exercise, where oxygen uptake and heart rate level off, energy demands and energy production are balanced, and the body can maintain the level of exertion for an extended period of time.

Stretch reflex is a protective contraction of the muscles being stretched. It is the body's defense against overstretch, and possible injury. Example: Knee jerk reflex (reaction to a tap on the quadriceps tendon below knee cap).

Stroke volume is the volume of blood pumped out of the heart (by the ventricles) in one contraction.

Submaximal is less than maximum. Submaximum exercise requires less than one's maximum oxygen uptake, heart rate or anaerobic power. Usually refers to intensity of the exercise, but may be used to refer to duration.

Target heart rate (THR) is the heart rate at which one aims to exercise. For example, the American College of Sports Medicine recommends that healthy adults exercise at a THR of 60–90 percent of maximum heart rate reserve.

Tendon is the fibrous connective tissue that connects muscle to bone.

Vein is a vessel which returns blood from the various parts of the body back to the heart.

VO2 Max is the Maximum Volume of Oxygen consumed per unit of time. In scientific notation, a dot appears over the V to indicate "per unit of time."

Warm up is the gradual increase in the intensity of exercise to allow physiological processes to prepare for greater energy outputs. Changes include: rise in body temperature, cardiovascular- and respiratory-system changes, increase in muscle elasticity and contractility, etc.

Related Websites

American Heart Association
www.amhrt.org

Runner's World
www.runnersworld.com

USA Triathlon
www.USATriathlon.org

American Running Association
www.americanrunning.org

Walking
www.walkingconnection.com

Cardiovascular Endurance
www.sport-fitness-advisor.com/endurancetraining
www.stretching.com
www.everydaychoices.org

Study Questions

Name ______________________________

1. Do you engage in any type of anaerobic activities? What are your signs or symptoms that you may be reaching an anaerobic threshold? Are there any after effects the next day? Why?

2. Where are the locations on your body that you can take your pulse? What are you really measuring or counting?

3. What are the three (3) components that the F.I.T. formula represent? How do they apply for improving your fitness level?

4. What are the target heart rate training zones at age 18? 25? 30? 35? Any difference between zones for men or women?

5. If a person is in excellent aerobic (cardio-respiratory) condition, would they do more or less physical activity to reach a heart rate of 140, as opposed to an inactive, sedentary person?

6. What did the heart rate *you* recorded during the aerobic fitness test (12 minute run/walk) mean to you in addition to the distance?

7. What are some of the causes of low back pain? How prevalent is this problem in the United States? Are any of them preventable?

Basics of Nutrition

KEY TERMS	
Amino acids	Nutrients
Calorie	Phytochemical
Carbohydrate	Polyunsaturated fat
Diet	Protein
Fat	RDA
Glucose	Saturated fat
Glycogen	Trans fat
Hypoglycemia	Unsaturated fat
Monounsaturated fat	Vitamins

Proper nutrition is essential for optimum health and fitness. Excesses of food are the biggest problem, such as saturated fats, cholesterol, refined foods, and all amount to a large increase in calories. This over indulgence of foods can cause obesity, heart disorders, cancer, hypertension, and kidney failure. Therefore, it is important to understand the basics of nutrition first.

The American Dietetic Association has found that coronary heart disease can be reversed by changes in diet and lifestyle. Diet is a factor in over 35% of all cancer cases. People with high blood pressure can alter this, more with a simple increase in potassium, rather than lowering their sodium intake. There are lower incidences of colon/endometrial cancers and heart disease with a higher consumption of whole-grain, fiber-rich foods. The environmental factors of having X-Rays, UV heat, cigarette smoke, alcohol, pollutants, and the ozone exposure are difficult, but we can improve the quality of our life and health with simple changes in our nutrition.

© DUSAN ZIDAR/Shutterstock.com

SIX BASIC NUTRIENTS	
Water	The most important nutrient. Our bodies are made up of over 60% water, and it is used for many chemical reactions. It stabilizes body temperature, carries nutrients to and waste away from cells, and is needed for cells to function.
Carbohydrates	Calories which provide energy for your muscles and your brain. Carbohydrates are the primary energy source when you are exercising hard. 45–60% of your calories should be carbohydrate-rich foods such as vegetables, fruits, breads, and grains.
Protein	Essential to build and repair the body's tissues, red blood cells, hair, and for synthesizing hormones. Protein is digested into amino acids. It can be used as fuel when inadequate carbohydrates are available, such as during exhausting exercise. 20–35% of your calories should be protein-rich foods such as fish, chicken, lean meats, and dried beans.
Fat	Necessary part of every cell; protects internal organs; carries fat-soluble vitamins. Fat is stored energy used during low-level activity. Animal fats tend to be saturated and contribute to heart disease, where vegetable fats like corn oil and olive oil are generally unsaturated and less harmful. You should limit your fat intake to no more than 20–35% of your daily calories.
Vitamins	Most vitamins are chemical substances and are metabolic catalysts that regulate reaction within the body. They include vitamins A, B complex, C, D, E, and K. Most vitamins should be obtained from a balanced diet.
Minerals	Regulate body processes. They are elements obtained from foods, that when combined form structures of the body, i.e., calcium in the bones. Important inerals are magnesium, phosphorus, sodium, potassium, and zinc.

Antioxidants will protect us against damage from free radicals. Free radicals are unstable compounds released as a by-product of oxidation in cellular metabolism. These antioxidants may play a role in preventing lung cancer, and reverse diet induced atherosclerosis, and heart attacks in men. The RDA recommends three vitamins and one mineral which are critical antioxidants. They are best found in foods, not taken in supplements.

Some people refer to these as the Fabulous Four:

Vitamin A—3,000 iu	(Beta Carotene is a precursor to Vitamin A) Sources: Carrots, sweet potatoes, peppers, apricots, dark green or yellow vegetables)
Vitamin C—60 mg	(Orange juice has lots of this & potassium) Sources: Red peppers, kiwi, broccoli, brussel sprouts, cauliflower, papaya, strawberry, oranges, grapefruit, cantalope)
Vitamin E—30 iu	(In most foods—supplements unnecessary) Sources: Fortified cereals, almonds, sunflower seeds, wheat germ, asparagus, spinach, tomatoes, peanuts, and peanut butter)
Selenium—Not Est.	(Enhances immune system & protects cells) Sources: Tuna, nuts, lean meats, & seafood)

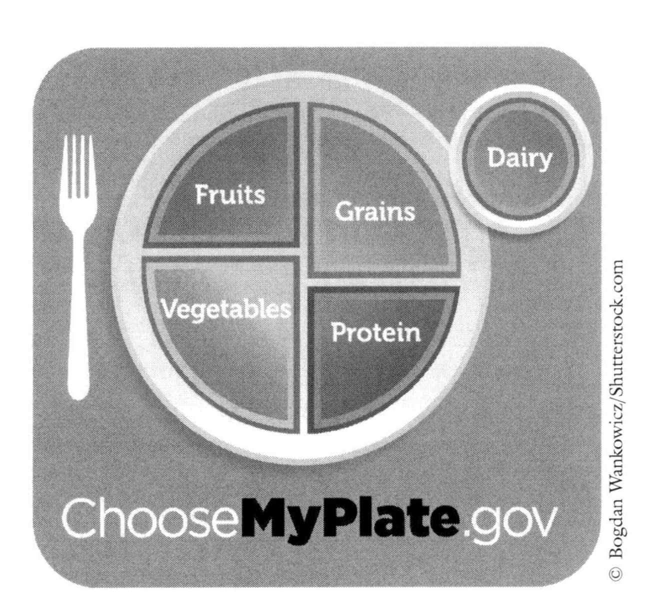

Cut back on sodium and empty calories from solid fats and added sugars. Look out for salt (sodium) in foods you buy. Compare sodium in foods and choose those with a lower number.

Drink water instead of sugary drinks. Eat sugary desserts less often. Limit empty calories to less than 260 per day, based on a 2,000 calorie diet.

Make foods that are high in solid fats—such as cakes, cookies, ice cream, pizza, cheese, sausages, and hot dogs—occasional choices, not every day foods.

NUTRITION NEWS

Calories per Gram of Food

1 gram of Carbohydrates	= 4 kcals
1 gram of Protein	= 4 kcals
1 gram of Alcohol	= 7 kcals
1 gram of Fat	= 9 kcals

Guidelines

- Be Consistent w/Calorie Intake
- Drink 8 glasses of fluid/Day (Half of which is water)
- If Low Calorie Diet for long, Take Vitamin Supplement

Suggestions to Decrease Fats in the Diet

- AVOID SATURATED FAT
- AVOID SUGARS AND SWEETS
- Avoid Fried and Fast Food
- Avoid Hidden Fats (Dips)
- Broil or Bake Foods
- Use Wine and Vinegar as Dressing
- Use more Yogurt and Skim Milk
- Use more Turkey Meat
- Use Extra Light or Whipped Margarine
- Use Low Fat Products
- Use more FISH in the Diet

KEYS TO NUTRITION

- Balance—Try to eat selections at each meal from fruits, vegetables, dairy, protein, and grains.
- Variety—Eat a variety of foods. There is no one magic food. Make eating fun, not the same routine.
- Moderation—Balance out nutrient-wise choices at each meal. Try selecting foods, eating less and healthier.
- Nutritionists believe plant-based eating will be the wave of the future. (**Phytochemicals** are plant foods)
- Omega-3 (DHA) are fatty acids contained in fish oils and wild game, and are believed to lower coronary heart disease, rheumatoid arthritis, and depression.
- In general, vegetables have more nutritional value than fruits.
- Caffeine increases the risk of cancer, high blood pressure, heart disease, and fibrocystic breast disease. Coffee drinkers who smoke have a greater risk of coronary heart disease.
- One cup of coffee with a hamburger reduces the iron absorption by 40%!

PHYTOCHEMICALS

Phytochemicals are super healthy plant compounds that research shows can help ward off many kinds of cancer, high cholesterol, heart disease and even cataracts. The best way to get these nutritional powerhouse compounds is to eat lots of vegetables, fruits, beans, grains and herbs.

Beta Carotene can help protect against lung cancer, heart disease and cataracts. *Lutein and Zeazanthin* stave off macular degeneration, a common cause of blindness in older adults. *Limonene* helps prevent breast cancer. *Quercetin* acts as an anti-inflammatory and can relieve allergies and fight infection. *Indoles and Organosulfurs* may block carcinogens that cause cancer. *Saponins* protect against high cholesterol. *Lycopene* seems to help fend off prostate and cervical cancer.

Phytochemical	Best Sources
Beta-Carotene	Carrots, sweet potatoes, red peppers, apricots, lettuce
Indoles	Broccoli, cauliflower, sprouts
Limonene	Green veggies
Lutein, Zeaxanthin	Citrus fruit peel, mint, thyme, caraway, coriander, cardamom Kale, collard greens, broccoli, spinach, tangerines, oranges
Lycopene	Tomatoes, pink grapefruit, guava, raspberries, strawberries
Organosulfurs	Garlic, onions, leeks, shallots
Quercetin	Tomatoes, oregano, apples, onions, lettuce
Saponins	Garlic, dried beans, oats, asparagus

ENERGY DRINKS

(Nutritional Supplements)

New products on the market for consumers such as energy drinks are being sold in record numbers in the new millennium. Many consumers, including athletes, may not understand the effects of many ingredients in these drinks, which contain one or more nervous system stimulants. Stimulants are any drugs that affect the central nervous system, which increase alertness, and decrease fatigue. Also reported were erratic behavior and unpleasant withdrawal symptoms, including depression. **Ingredients to be aware of are: caffeine, ephedra (ma huang), ginseng, and guarana.**

About Guarana

Guarana has recently become a popular ingredient in energy drinks and teas. Guarana is one of the richest sources of caffeine, containing up to three times the amount of caffeine as coffee. The amount of caffeine does not have to be listed on guarana drinks. People with heart conditions, diabetes, high blood pressure, epilepsy, overactive thyroid, anxiety, insomnia, and kidney disease should only use guarana under doctor's supervision. Serious effects have been reported when combined with products containing ephedra. It may increase the risk of stroke, hemorrhage, myocardial infarction, and sudden death along with increases in heart rate, blood pressure, and potentially harmful changes in glucose and potassium levels.

FACTS ABOUT OUR BODY'S FUEL

Carbohydrates (45–60% of Daily Intake)

Carbohydrates are our best energy source. Breakfast is our most important meal of the day. It increases our concentration, our efficiency, our patience, and our energy. People that skip breakfast, tend to have more struggles with their weight. Cereals that have high fiber, and fortified with iron, are good starters. Other quick fixes are: yogurt, bananas, blender drinks, raisins, bran muffins, & bagels.

Simple carbohydrates would be monosaccharides, disaccharides, and others that end in –ose, like fructose, sucrose. Simple carbohydrates provide energy, but contain no vitamins. Polymer carbohydrates provide energy also, but unless fortified, contain no vitamins or minerals. All sugars are converted into glucose for energy. **Complex carbohydrates** are starches such as plant foods. Good choices are: carrot sticks, wheat crackers, V8 juice, fruit, pretzels, peanuts, and seeds. Complex carbohydrates provide energy AND vitamins AND minerals. These starches you eat are digested into glucose, then either burned for energy or stored. People store extra dietary sugars in the form of muscle glycogen and liver glycogen.

Hypoglycemia (low blood sugar) sometimes occurs when you exercise too much, or have insufficient food. You may feel light headed, easily fatigued, have blurred vision, and be indecisive. It is important to have recovery carbohydrates within 1 to 4 hours after exercise. Depleted muscles need about 2 days to refuel after exhaustive exercise. Some of the best choices for recovery foods are: Potato (750 mg Potassium); Yogurt (500 mg); Banana (500 mg); Orange juice (420 mg); Pineapple juice (360); Raisins (300 mg); and lastly, Gatorade (24 mg).

Carbohydrates and the Glycemic Index of Foods

Carbohydrates should be the primary source for energy in your diet. Some carbohydrates give you a quick energy boost, like sports drinks, and energy bars. Other sources of carbohydrates such as barley or lentils, are better if you want energy in an hour or more.

The Glycemic Index (GI), rates foods by how fast or slow their carbohydrates break down to increase blood glucose levels. Glucose itself is rated at 100, and everything else is compared to this standard. When you would like a quick energy boost for your muscles, choose foods with a GI of 60 to 100. When you need something small before working out choose foods with a GI less than 60.

These food values apply to foods eaten alone. Any added protein or fat, slows the digestion of carbohydrates and will lead to a slower release of blood glucose.

GLYCEMIC INDEX OF FOODS			
Glucose	100	Pasta	50
Potato	98	Oatmeal	49
Carrots (cooked)	92	Orange Juice	46
Honey	87	Orange	43
Corn Flakes	83	Grapes	43
White Rice	72	Whole Wheat Pasta	42
Whole Wheat Bread	72	Rye Bread	42
White Bread	69	Apple	39
Raisins	64	Kidney Beans	33
Banana	61	Lentils	29
Soft Roll	58	Barley	22
Corn	58	Carrot (Raw)	16
Peas & All Bran	51		

FOOD LABELING REFERENCE TABLES

The FDA uses Daily Values (DVs) for food labeling. DVs for the following macronutrients are Daily Reference Values (DRVs). The DV's used by the FDA for vitamins and minerals are the RDIs listed here. For people 4 years or older, eating 2,000 calories per day, the RDIs are:

Total FAT	**65 g**
Saturated Fatty Acids	20 g
Cholesterol	300 mg
Sodium	2400 mg
Potassium	4700 mg
Total CARBOHYDRATE	**300 g**
Fiber	25 g
Total PROTEIN	**50 g**

Vitamin A	**3000 IU**
Vitamin B6	**2 mg**
Vitamin B12	**6 ug**
Vitamin C	**60 mg**
Vitamin D	**400 IU**
Vitamin E	**30 IU**
Vitamin K	**80 ug**
Calcium/Phosphorus	**1000 mg**
Iron/Zinc	**18/15 mg**

Proteins (20–35% of Daily Intake)

Amino acids are building blocks. Therefore, it is important to combine grains with milk products; grains with beans; and legumes with seeds. Some people try to substitute protein powders for food. An example would be buying 5 Tbs. of protein power for $1.10, when you could have a $3\frac{1}{2}$ oz. can of tuna for half the price! Animal protein contains all 9 essential amino acids, called "complete proteins". Vegetables are incomplete proteins. Vegetarians usually lack protein in their diet, so it is important to watch your intake.

Protective benefits of protein include: Assurance of proper muscle development; Reducing the risk of iron-deficiency anemia; and improvement in healing. You don't have to eat beef to get plenty of protein, but animal products generally provide the highest quality protein. Vegetable sources should be combined with animal proteins to enhance their quality.

An excellent source of protein is found in meat. Some people feel meat is bad for you. Meat is not bad, the fat in the meat is! Lean meat contains lots of iron (to prevent anemia), and zinc (to help with healing). People that have iron deficiency anemia, feel tired, and usually have lower performance. Women athletes are more vulnerable, especially during menstruation. Many athletes are told that protein and amino acid supplements will build more muscle and add to their performance. There is no evidence that supports this claim.

Fats (20–35% of Daily Intake)

Eat less fat! When you look at a food label, note the grams of fat, but also read the ingredients to see what type of fat the food contains. The following chart helps to identify needed grams of fat.

Calorie Needs Per Day	Grams of Fat for 25% Fat Intake
1,200	35
1,500	40
1,800	50
2,000	55
2,400	65
2,600	70

TRANS FAT

A trans fat, also called a trans fatty acid or transunsaturated fat, is an unsaturated fat that is artificially saturated with hydrogen—hydrogenated. Food manufacturers hydrogenate unsaturated fats to make them hard at room temperature. Margarine and vegetable shortening are the best examples, although many food products have "hydrogenated oils" on their labels. (One margarine on the market, *Smart Balance*, has no trans fat, or hydrogenated oils.) The American Heart Association supports a proposal by the Food and Drug Administration to include the amounts of trans fat, be added to food labels.

The reason saturated fats—and now trans fats—get a bad rap is that they raise levels of LDL in the blood. In fact, saturated fats have a greater effect on raising blood levels of cholesterol than cholesterol you get in your diet. And, trans fats, according to a recently published report by the New England Journal of Medicine, not only raise the LDL level, they appear to lower HDL levels and raise triglyceride levels as well. Trans fats also raise our heart disease risk when eaten in excess.

In a Harvard study, scientists estimate that trans fats are responsible for between 30,000 to 100,000 premature coronary heart disease deaths every year! Gram for gram, they say, trans fats are twice as bad for us as saturated fats. Other scientists think the two fat types are roughly equivalent.

Limit pies, cookies, snack cakes, doughnuts, and crackers. Foods loaded with trans fats and saturated fats are french fries, and fried chicken.

Example: French Fries (Lg.—5 oz.) 24 g Total Fat, 6 g Saturated Fat, 7 g Trans Fat (Nearly 40% of artery clogging fat)

Hamburger (Lg.—7 oz.) 36 g Total Fat, 14 g Saturated Fat, 3 g Trans Fat (Nearly 47% of artery clogging fat)

Potato Skins (Lg.—12 oz.) 95 g Total Fat, 41 g Saturated Fat, 8 g Trans Fat (Nearly 68% of artery clogging fat)

The American Heart Association allows 30% of daily calories to come from fat, but active people should keep fat intake to 25%.

Sources of Saturated Fat

Saturated fat in the diet, raises blood levels of artery-clogging cholesterol. Most Americans have too much saturated fat and not enough whole grains, fruits, and vegetables. Another type of harmful type of dietary fat—**trans fat**—comes from sources such as margarine, baked goods, and snacks. **The following is a breakdown of sources of saturated fat in the American diet:**

39% Meat, fish, and poultry
34% Fats and oils
20% Dairy products
3% Other
2% Legumes and nuts
2% Eggs

SERVING SIZE

Is your serving the same size as the one on the label? If you eat double the serving size listed, you need to double the nutrient and calorie values. If you eat one-half the serving size shown here, cut the nutrient and calorie values in half.

CALORIES

Are you overweight? Cut back a little on calories! Look here to see how a serving of the food adds to your daily total. A 5′ 4″, 138-lb. active woman needs about 2,200 calories each day. A 5′ 10″, 174-lb. active man needs about 2,900. How about you?

TOTAL CARBOHYDRATE

When you cut down on fat, you can eat more carbohydrates. Carbohydrates are in foods like bread, potatoes, fruits and vegetables. Choose these often! They give you more nutrients than **sugars** like soda pop and candy.

DIETARY FIBER

Grandmother called it "roughage," but her advice to eat more is still up-to-date! That goes for both soluble and insoluble kinds of dietary fiber. Fruits, vegetables, whole-grain foods, beans and peas are all good sources and can help reduce the risk of heart disease and cancer.

PROTEIN

Most Americans get more protein than they need. Where there is animal protein, there is also fat and cholesterol. Eat small servings of lean meat, fish and poultry. Use skim or low-fat milk, yogurt and cheese. Try vegetable proteins like beans, grains and cereals.

VITAMINS & MINERALS

Your goal here is 100% of each for the day. Don't count on one food to do it all. Let a combination of foods add up to a winning score.

Nutrition Facts

Serving Size 1/4 Cup (30g)
Servings Per Container About 38

Amount Per Serving	
Calories 200 Calories from Fat 150	
	% Daily Value*
Total Fat 17g	**26%**
Saturated Fat 2.5g	**13%**
Trans Fat 0g	
Cholesterol 0mg	**0%**
Sodium 120mg	**5%**
Total Carbohydrate 7g	**2%**
Dietary Fiber 2g	**8%**
Sugars 1g	
Protein 5g	
Vitamin A 0% • Vitamin C 0%	
Calcium 4% • Iron 8%	

*Percent Daily Values are based on a 2,000 calorie diet.

More nutrients may be listed on some labels

TOTAL FAT

Aim low: Most people need to cut back on fat! Too much fat may contribute to heart disease and cancer. Try to limit your **calories from fat**. For a healthy heart, choose foods with a big difference between the total number of calories and the number of calories from fat.

SATURATED FAT

A new kind of fat? No—saturated fat is part of the total fat in food. It is listed separately because it's the key player in raising blood cholesterol and your risk of heart disease. Eat less!

CHOLESTEROL

Too much cholesterol—a second cousin to fat—can lead to heart disease. Challenge yourself to eat less than 300 mg each day.

SODIUM

You call it "salt," the label calls it "sodium." Either way, it may add up to high blood pressure in some people. So, keep your sodium intake low—2,400 to 3,000 mg or less each day.*

*The AHA recommends no more than 3,000 mg sodium per day for healthy adults.

DAILY VALUE

Feel like you're drowning in numbers? Let the Daily Value be your guide. Daily Values are listed for people who eat 2,000 or 2,500 calories each day. If you eat more, your personal daily value may be higher than what's listed on the label. If you eat less, your personal daily value may be lower.

For fat, saturated fat, cholesterol and sodium, choose foods with a low % **Daily Value**. For total carbohydrate, dietary fiber, vitamins and minerals, your daily value goal is to reach 100% of each.

g = grams (About 28 g = 1 ounce)

mg = milligrams (1,000 mg = 1 g)

THE HEALTHY EATING PYRAMID

Department of Nutrition, Harvard School of Public Health

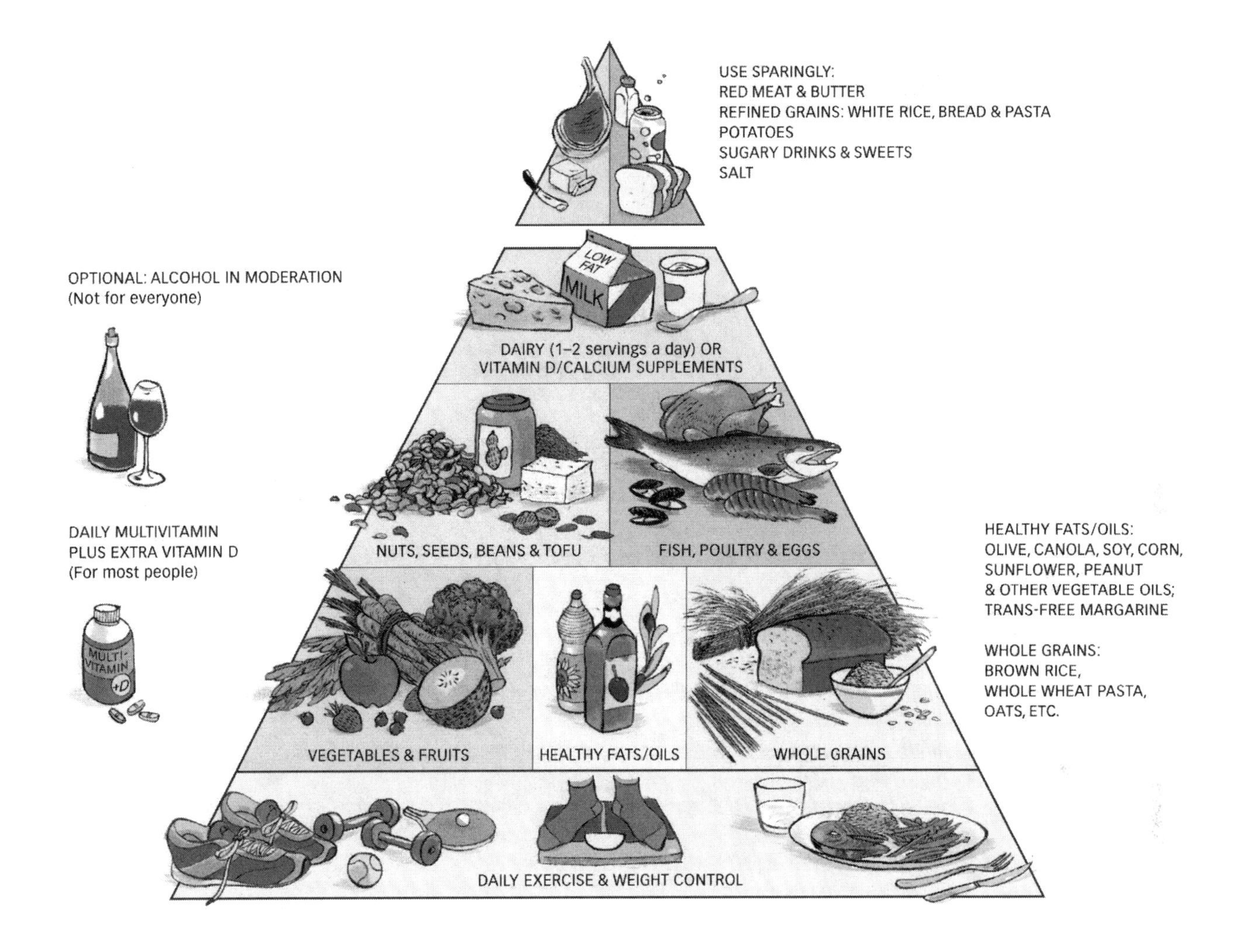

For more information about the Healthy Eating Pyramid:

WWW.THE NUTRITION SOURCE.ORG

Eat, Drink, and Be Healthy
by Walter C. Willett, M.D. and Patrick J. Skerrett (2005)
Free Press/Simon & Schuster Inc.

HEALTHY PEOPLE 2020

Nutrition and Weight Status

Objectives Retained from 2010

1. Increase the proportion of adults who are at a healthy weight.
2. Reduce the proportion of adults who are obese.
3. Reduce iron deficiency among young children and females of childbearing age.
4. Reduce iron deficiency among pregnant females.
5. Reduce the proportion of children and adolescents who are overweight or obese.
6. Increase the contribution of fruits to the diets of the population aged 2 years and older.
7. Increase the variety and contribution of vegetables to the diets of the population aged 2 years and older.
8. Increase the contribution of whole grains to the diets of the population aged 2 years and older.
9. Reduce consumption of saturated fat in the population aged 2 years and older.
10. Reduce consumption of sodium in the population aged 2 years and older.
11. Increase consumption of calcium in the population aged 2 years and older.
12. Increase the proportion of worksheets that offer nutrition or weight management classes or counseling.
13. Increase the proportion of physician offices visits that include counseling or education related to nutrition or weight.
14. Eliminate very low food security among children in U.S. households.

Objectives New for 2020

1. Prevent inappropriate weight gain in youth and adults.
2. Increase the proportion of primary care physicians who regularly measure the body mass index of their patients.
3. Reduce consumption of calories from solid fats and added sugars in the population aged 2 years and older.
4. Increase the number of states that have state-level policies that incentivize food retail outlets to provide foods that are encouraged by the Dietary Guidelines.
5. Increase the number of states with nutrition standards for foods and beverages provided to preschool-aged children in childcare.
6. Increase the percentage of schools that offer nutritious foods and beverages outside of school meals.

Source: Office of Disease Prevention & Health Promotion. U.S. Department of Health and Human Services
(Full document available at: www.healthypeople.gov/HP2020)

WORKSHEET 3

NAME ______________________

POINTS ______________ **RATING** ______________

Fat Intake

YOUR FAT SCORE: DO YOU . . . ?	RARELY	OFTEN	ALMOST ALWAYS
Choose lean meat, chicken, or fish?	1	5	10
Eat high-fat meats like bacon, lunch meats, or sausage?	10	5	1
Limit eggs to four yolks per week?	1	5	10
Read labels and select foods with less than three grams of fat per serving?	1	5	10
Choose low-fat or nonfat dairy products?	1	5	10
Limit fried foods?	1	5	10
Choose doughnuts, croissants, or sweet rolls for breakfast?	10	5	1
Choose reduced-fat or fat-free products when they are available?	1	5	10
Limit margarine, butter, salad dressings and sauces on foods?	1	5	10
Balance a high-fat dinner with a low-fat breakfast and lunch?	1	5	10

RATING

80+ Points = Excellent (Keep up the good work!)
60–79 Points = Fair (You're on your way)
10–59 Points = Poor (You can do better!)

TOTAL POINTS ______________

(COMPLETE THE OTHER SIDE)

DAILY DIET SUMMARY/CALORIC INTAKE

This form will be completed by writing down everything that you consume in **one day**. This includes food and beverages. These calories will make up your daily caloric intake. Make note the calories per serving and how many servings your consumed based on the food items label.

	Food	Servings	Calories
Breakfast	Example: cereal	2	400
	Non fat milk	2	250
	Beverage		

	Food	Servings	Calories
Snack			

	Food	Servings	Calories
Lunch			
	Beverage		

	Food	Servings	Calories
Snack			

	Food	Servings	Calories
Dinner			
	Beverage		

	Food	Servings	Calories
Dessert			

Total calories consumed for the day: ______________________________

(add up all of the calories coloumn)

Caloric expenditure: ______________________________

(the calories you burn throughout the day)*

* You can find your caloric expenditure at **www.nutritiondata.com.** Go to the **Tools link** and then click on the **Daily needs calculator**.

Glossary of Terms

Amino acids are the building blocks of protein. Twenty different amino acids are required by the body.

Calorie is used as a unit of metabolism (as in diet and energy expenditure) equals 1,000 small calories, and is often spelled with a capital C to make that distinction. It is the energy required to raise the temperature of one kilogram of water one degree Celsius. Also called a kilocalorie (kcal).

Carbohydrate is a chemical compound of carbon, oxygen, and hydrogen, usually with the hydrogen and oxygen in the right proportions to form water. Common forms are starches, sugars, cellulose and gums. Carbohydrates are more readily used for energy production than are fats and proteins.

Diet is the food one eats. May or may not be a selection of foods to accomplish a particular health or fitness objective.

Electrolytes are salts of the body such as sodium, potassium, magnesium, calcium and chloride.

Fat 1) A white or yellowish tissue which stores reserve energy, provides padding for organs and smooth body contours, 2) A compound of glycerol and various fatty acids. Dietary fat is not as readily converted to energy as are carbohydrates.

Glucose is blood sugar. The transportable form of carbohydrate, which reaches the cells.

Glycogen is the storage form of carbohydrate. Glycogen is used in the muscles for the production of energy.

Hypoglycemia is an abnormally low level of glucose in the blood (low blood sugar). May lead to shakiness, cold sweats, goose-bumps, hypothermia, hallucinations, strange behavior and, in extreme cases, convulsions and coma.

Monounsaturated fat is dietary fat whose molecules have one double bond open to receive more hydrogen. Found in many nuts, olive oil and avocados.

Nutrients are food and its specific elements and compounds that can be used by the body to build and maintain itself and to produce energy.

Phytochemicals refers to a wide variety of compounds produced by plants. These compounds can help ward off many kinds of cancer, high cholesterol, heart disease, and even cataracts.

Polyunsaturated fat is a dietary fat whose molecules have more than one double bond open to receive more hydrogen. Found in safflower oil, corn oil, soybeans, sesame seeds, sunflower seeds.

Protein are compounds of amino acids that make up most of the body's cells and perform other physiological functions.

RDA (Recommended Dietary Allowance) is the protein, vitamin and mineral amounts considered adequate to meet the nutrition needs of 98 percent of the healthy population. Established by the National Research Council of the National Academy of Sciences. The RDA is calculated to exceed the needs of most people.

Saturated fat is fat that contains glycerol and saturated fatty acids, found in high quantities in animal products (such as meat, milk, butter, and cheese) and in low quantities in vegetable products; high intake is associated with elevated blood cholesterol levels. They are usually hard at room temperature.

Trans fat is created when manufacturers partially hydrogenate liquid oils to make them more solid, more stable, and less greasy-tasting. Trans fat raises blood cholesterol, and therefore, the risk of heart disease.

Unsaturated fat is a dietary fat whose molecules have one or more double bonds open to receive more hydrogen atoms. Replacing saturated fats with unsaturated fats in the diet can help reduce cholesterol levels.

Vitamins are a number of unrelated organic substances that are required in trace amounts for the metabolic processes of the body and which occur in small amounts in many foods.

Related Websites

Tufts Health & Nutrition Letter
www.tuftshealthletter.com

Nutrition
www.nutrition.about.com
www.nutrition.com
www.foodinsight.org

Vegetarian Resource Group
www.vrg.org

American College of Nutrition
www.am-coll-nutr.org
Natl. Agricultural Lib.fnic.nal.usda.gov

Nutritional Professionals
www.dallasdietitian.com
www.mealsforyou.com
www.healthyeating.net
www.vegsource.com
www.healthy.net
www.dietitian.com

Study Questions

Name ______________________________

1. How much of the most important nutrient do *you* need daily? How much do *you* average per day? If not enough, what possible health problems could arise?

2. What are the recommended dietary goals of the nutrients that contain calories?

3. Do *you* know how to read food labels to determine the nutritional values of the food? What is the method of determining the percentage of fat?

4. What are phytochemicals? Which ones do you like in your diet?

5. Explain what is harmful about transfat, the hidden fat in foods?

Body Composition and Weight Management

KEY TERMS

Adipose tissue	Ketosis
Anorexia	Lean body mass
Body composition	Metabolism
Cellulite	Obesity
Fat-free weight	Spot Reducing

BODY COMPOSITION

Knowing what you weigh is one thing, but getting a reasonable idea of how much of your weight is body fat ranks as a better gauge of your risk of health problems. **Body composition** basically means how much of your body weight comes from fat mass, and how much comes from lean body mass (LBM).

Body fat consists of essential fat from cells, and protection of some internal organs, and storage fat for excess energy. Lean body mass consists of tissues, (primarily muscle tissue; heart, liver, kidneys and other organs), other than body fat. The adult body weight is composed of about 60% water. Lean body mass is the primary determinant of the body's basal metabolism rate, and is the major influence on one's energy requirements and nutrient needs.

Body composition is influenced by factors such as sex, age, diet, and exercise. Physical exercise can significantly influence body composition by helping to build muscle and lose fat. The primary effects of diet on our body's composition takes quite some time, but diet will affect our body in the short run when water is restricted or fasting takes place. Chronic overeating will definitely increase our fat stores.

You are **overfat** if you have an excess of fat weight, not lean body weight. **Overweight** refers to people with body weight 10% in excess of the standard height-weight tables. Some experts designate people being **obese** if body weight is more than 20% over standard, or an excessive accumulation of body fat. (Men > 25%—Women >30%)

Obesity frequently results in significant impairment of health. There is a higher risk of heart attack due to the increased strain excess body weight places on the heart and circulatory system. The heart must work harder, and the efficiency is reduced due to the accumulation of fat in the connective tissue beneath the membrane that encloses the heart. High blood pressure is very common among obese and overweight people. There is a reduction in the size of the arteries. The narrowing of arteries due to the accumulation of fat in the form of cholesterol or triglycerides (atherosclerosis) is a primary cause of coronary heart attacks, strokes, and crippling disability. Excess fat is the end result of an imbalance between the number of calories consumed and the number of calories expended to sustain basal needs and daily activities. Other factors add to obesity issues.

Genetic inheritance influences chances of becoming fat more than most any other factor. There is approximately a 40% chance if one parent is obese, you will also become obese. However, it is still within our power to control our body composition—increase our lean body mass, and decrease our fat mass!

STANDARDS FOR FATNESS (PERCENT BODY FAT)

Classification	Men	Women
Essential Fat	No Less Than 5%	No Less Than 8%
Borderline	5%–8%	8%–11%
Desirable (Athletes)	8%–9%	12%–15%
Desirable (Good Health)	10%–20%	16%–26%
Marginal Zone	21%–25%	27%–32%
Overfatness (Obesity)	More Than 25%	More Than 32%

Health Consequences of Obesity According to the Surgeon General's Report 2010, obesity in early life has been found to increase the risk for various diseases in adulthood, including diabetes and heart disease, in part because obese children are likely to become obese adults. Several studies have also found short-term effects of excess weight during childhood—for example, high BMI levels among children and teenagers are associated with childhood development of atherosclerosis.

The growing U.S. obesity epidemic is reflected in the tripling, since 1980, of the number of Americans who have diabetes. Approximately 8% of U.S. adults have type 2 diabetes, a disease that increases the risk for cardiovascular disease, stroke, kidney disease, blindness, lower-limb amputation, and other problems. Obesity is the most important risk factor for type 2 diabetes.

Height (in feet and inches), without shoes	Weight in pounds, without clothes Age 19–34	Weight in pounds, without clothes Age 35+
5' 0"	97–128	108–138
5' 1"	101–132	111–143
5' 2"	104–137	115–148
5' 3"	107–141	119–152
5' 4"	111–146	122–157
5' 5"	114–150	126–162
5' 6"	118–155	130–167
5' 7"	121–160	134–172
5' 8"	125–164	138–178
5' 9"	129–169	142–183
5' 10"	132–174	146–188
5' 11"	136–179	151–194
6' 0"	140–184	155–199
6' 1"	144–189	159–205
6' 2"	148–195	164–210
6' 3"	152–200	168–216
6' 4"	156–205	173–222
6' 5"	160–211	177–228
6' 6"	164–216	182–234

Standard height-weight charts have been the norm for estimating what a reasonable weight should be for a given age and gender. At best these charts are just the average of what others weigh rather than realistic weights for specific individuals. These height-weight charts are inadequate to determine if a person is physically fit. Muscle weighs more than fat, so a person could in fact weigh more than a chart may recommend, but be ideal as far as body fat percentage. People assume if they lose weight on a scale at home it is fat loss. Many times what people see, is water loss for the most part. It's important for individuals to know their percentage of body fat.

MEASURING BODY FAT

To determine how much of your body is made up of fat, there are many different ways of measurement. As mentioned earlier, height-weight charts are not a reliable way to measure body composition. Measuring body fat remains an inexact science. Currently, it is only an estimate of fat mass vs. fat-free mass.

Direct Measurement Techniques

Radiologic Measurement, uses a computer to measure body composition. Computed tomography (CT), magnetic resonance imaging (MRI), or ultrasonography are three common procedures currently being performed. MRI has about a 5% margin of error in persons with 30% or more body fat. Ultrasound costs less and has a lower risk, but is less accurate than either CT or MRI.

Isotope Dilution estimates the amount of total body water and in turn fat-free mass by having people drink water with tracers, then measure the levels in saliva, urine or breath for calculations, with a potential error of 2–9%.

Hydrostatic Underwater Weighing is based on the principle that body volume correlates with the loss of weight in the water. Individuals being measured are submerged in a tank and underwater weight is recorded. This is done 5–10 times, then the 3 heaviest reading are then averaged and used in a set of equations to calculate body fat. (Residual lung volume must also be measured). Error ranges from 2–3%, and less accurate with women, children, older adults, well-trained athletes, and African Americans, due to variations in the density of fat-free mass.

Indirect Measurement Techniques

Bioelectrical Impedance Analysis (BIA) is very common and easy to measure, and involves passing a painless current of electricity through the body. Lean tissue (composed mainly of water) readily conducts the applied current, whereas fat acts as an insulator and conducts little current. Values obtained through BIA are plugged into age-, sex-, and fatness-specific equations to calculate percent body fat and percent lean body mass. People being measured must be properly hydrated and should abstain from exercise and alcohol prior to testing. (Other considerations: Edema, Electrolyte Imbalance, Extreme Dehydration, Metabolic Disorder, Heart/Kidney Dysfunction, Extremes in body temperature, Extreme Obesity, and Cancer).

Waist-to-Hip Ratio Waist circumference divided by hip circumference, provides a good marker of cardiovascular disease risk. This will be done in the lab assignment to find out if you are an apple or a pear? Most men are apples, because they are wide around the belly and chest. Most women are pears, because they are wider around the hips and thighs. Apples have a far greater risk of developing heart disease and high blood pressure, high blood sugar, and high insulin. Pears suffer more from varicose veins and knee problems, which have to support their heavier hips. You can't go from being an apple to being a pear, or vice versa, but since most people lose weight from their upper bodies faster than from their lower bodies, you can become less of an apple or a thinner pear, simply by taking off some pounds.

Waist Circumference

Fat located inside the abdominal wall (visceral fat) contributes more to the risk of cardiovascular disease and diabetes than does fat in other areas of the body (subcutaneous fat). Some experts suggest waist circumference may be a better predictor of health risk from cardiovascular disease. Standards are:

- Men: No greater than 102 cm (40 inches)
- Women: No greater than 88 cm (34.6 inches)
- Post-menopausal women: No greater than 110 cm (43.3 inches)

	Men	Men	Women	Women
RISK	cm	inches	cm	Inches
Very High	>120	>47	>110	>43.5
High	100-120	39.5-47	90-109	35.5-43
Low	80-99	31.5-39	70-89	28.5-35
Very Low	<80	<31.5	<70	<38.5

Body Mass Index (BMI) is a number which estimates whether your body fat is high enough to put you at risk for such chronic conditions as heart disease and diabetes. BMI is calculated by dividing weight in kilograms by height in meters squared. (BMI's may not be "fat"—bodybuilders weight is mostly muscle and may score high on BMI charts, even though the proportion of body fat is low.) There is some difference as to the exact cut-off point for unhealthy BMI, but the following chart should help you.

BMI	19	20	21	22	23	24	25	26	27	28	29	30
	Generally Healthy				Healthy				Unhealthy			
4′10″	91	96	100	105	110	115	119	124	129	134	138	143
4′11″	94	99	104	109	114	119	124	128	133	138	143	148
5′	97	102	107	112	118	123	128	133	138	143	148	153
5′1″	100	106	111	116	122	127	132	137	143	148	153	158
5′2″	104	109	115	120	126	131	136	142	147	153	158	164
5′3″	107	113	118	124	130	135	141	146	152	158	163	169
5′4″	110	116	122	128	134	140	145	151	157	163	168	174
5′5″	114	120	126	132	138	144	150	156	162	168	174	180
5′6″	118	124	130	136	142	148	155	161	167	173	179	186
5′7″	121	127	134	140	146	153	159	166	172	178	185	191
5′8″	125	131	138	144	151	158	164	171	177	184	190	197
5′9″	128	135	142	149	155	162	169	176	182	189	196	203
5′10″	132	139	146	153	160	167	174	181	188	195	202	207
5′11″	136	143	150	157	165	172	179	186	193	200	208	215
6′	140	147	154	162	169	177	184	191	199	206	213	221
6′1″	144	151	159	166	174	182	189	197	204	212	219	227
6′2″	148	155	163	171	179	186	194	202	210	218	225	233
6′3″	142	160	168	176	184	192	200	208	216	224	232	240
6′4″	156	164	172	180	189	197	205	213	221	230	238	246
Height	Weight (in pounds)											

Skinfold Measurements are the most common for estimating body fat. Accuracy depends on the examiner's experience and the number of sites measured; the margin for error for skilled examiners range from 3–5%, but can be higher with extremes of body fat. Skinfolds are measured on the right side of the body with a set of calipers. Only the skin and adipose tissue will be measured at three sites. These measurements will be done in the lab and are good predictions of body fat.

Five Major Effects of Exercise in Reducing Weight and Fat

1. Increase Total Daily Energy Expenditure
2. Enhances Fat Mobilization & Maintenance of Lean Body Mass
3. Reduces Upper Body and Abdominal Visceral Fat
4. Increases Rate and Amount of Fat Metabolized
5. Reduces the Mortality Rate in Obese Persons

Physical Activity Guidelines for Americans
Adults (aged 18-64)

- Adults should do 2 hours and 30 minutes a week of moderate-intensity, or 1 hour and 15 minutes (75 minutes) a week of vigorous-intensity aerobic physical activity, or an equivalent combination of moderate- and vigorous-intensity aerobic physical activity. Aerobic activity should be performed in episodes of at least 10 minutes, preferably spread throughout the week.
- Additional health benefits are provided by increasing to 5 hours (300 minutes) a week of moderate-intensity aerobic physical activity, or 2 hours and 30 minutes a week or vigorous-intensity physical activity, or an equivalent combination of both.
- Adults should also do muscle-strengthening activities that involve all major muscle groups performed on two or more days per week.

Source: U.S. Dept. of Health & Human Services. (www.health.gov)

Facts about Body Fat

- 75 Billion fat cells are normal. This varies with each person.
- You can shrink the *size* of the fat cells, but they will *not* go away.
- Fat cells will increase in number with obesity, age, and inactivity.
- Creeping obesity—Most people will gain 1 lb./yr. after age 25.
- Metabolism slows down without activity. Daily exercise is *critical!*
- For every liter of oxygen consumed, 5 calories of fat are burned.

WEIGHT MANAGEMENT

Since 1993, estimates are that 65% of adults are overweight. Nearly one in four adults follows weight-loss programs. A decrease in physical activity usually accompanies age. "Creeping obesity" is a term used as people grow older, who exercise less and calorie consumption does not vary. Most Americans between 30–60 years of age are overfat. Obesity increases health problems, and death by 15–20%. Diabetes mellitis, hyperlipidemia (high cholesterol and triglyceride levels), and high blood pressure are known to be related or due to obesity, while coronary heart disease, cirrhosis of the liver, chronic lung disease, and emotional disorders may be aggravated by an overweight condition.

Studies from the American Medical Association suggest several possibilities as to why people are overweight:

1. High standard of living
2. Mechanization
3. Relative abundance of leisure time
4. Lack of physical activity
5. Insufficient knowledge about weight control
6. Lack of motivation with regard to weight control

Many years ago our ancestors strived for survival—their lifestyle was very active as they hunted for food, made preparations for shelter, and traveled long distances. Today, we are far less active, and most people consume high levels of fat—therefore, obesity and weight management is a major concern.

The public spends millions of dollars each year in the weight loss industry. There are many quick fix diet programs, pills, even surgeries—but at what cost? What are the side effects? How far are you willing to go to achieve the desired results? Why not learn more about weight management—the background, the theories, the best way to achieve lifelong fitness, health, and happiness?

Literature shows that 1) not everybody who thinks she or he needs to lose weight really does need to (there is a difference between need and desire), and 2) not everybody can maintain desired weight loss. People who achieve prolonged weight loss are in the minority. Behavior and lifestyle changes are dependent on factors such as gender, genetics, and childhood. An individual's weight fluctuation depends on a number of predetermined factors:

1. Resting metabolic rate (RMR)
2. Fat-metabolizing enzyme activity
3. Set point theory
4. Fat cell number

Resting Metabolic Rate (RMR) is defined as the energy expended while resting. Basal metabolic rate (BMR) is also another synonymous term. This metabolic rate is directly related to oxygen consumption. For every liter of oxygen consumed, about 5 calories are burned. Lean body mass uses a higher amount of oxygen than fat mass. Our metabolic rate is dependent on our body composition and our level of activity.

People that are sedentary have low RMRs and have four times the chance of gaining weight as those people who have high RMRs. Some studies indicate that heredity has much to do with our metabolic rate, as mentioned earlier in this chapter. In general, women need about 1,200 calories per day and men need about 1,600 for BMR functions.

Factors Affecting Basal Metabolic Rate

1. *Age*—Usually the younger the person, the higher BMR. After age 20, BMR decreases 2% per decade throughout life.
2. *Height*—Tall and thin people generally have higher BMRs. Leaner people metabolize calories at a higher rate.

3. *Gender*—Men normally have a 10–15% faster metabolic rate than women. Leaner tissue uses more calories—and women usually have less lean tissue and higher body fat.
4. *Dieting*—Metabolic rates drop as low as 20% during fasting. Lower BMRs conserves fat stores and hinders weight loss.
5. *Environmental Temperature*—BMR is higher in heat and cold. People living in warmer climates have 5–20% higher BMRs. Cold and muscular shivering also stimulates your BMR.
6. *Exercise*—Can increase your metabolic rate and depending on the type of exercise, may stay elevated hours after the activity.

Fat-Metabolizing Enzymes which are responsible for clearing fatty acids from the bloodstream and depositing them into the fat cell, are called LPLs—Lipoprotein lipase. Higher levels of LPL may cause hunger in obese people and enhance fat formation. LPL levels differ in individuals. It could be that some people produce more LPL than normal and have more potential for obesity, as some research suggests.

Set Point Theory is a term used by some scientists, and may be considered controversial—but basically, is a belief that the brain and body automatically set the body's weight or fat percentage regardless of our efforts to change the body composition. This control system regulates how much we eat and the fat we accumulate. This may be why people respond differently to weight-loss programs.

Fat-Cells vary from 25 billion in lean people to 50 billion in mildly obese, and about 273 billion in the severely obese. Once new fat cells have developed, if the person loses his/her fat weight, the fat cells decrease in size, not the number of fat cells. Therefore, if children become obese at an early age, it may be more difficult to manage their weight as they grow to adults, and have a continuing weight problem. As mentioned earlier in this chapter, energy is best expressed in calories. **One pound of body fat is equal to 3,500 calories. Calories count significantly in losing fat.**

Calories in = Calories expended = Weight maintained
Calories in > Calories expanded = Weight gain
Calories in < Calories expended = Weight loss

Met Rate (Metabolic Rate) is defined as 3.5 ml/kg/minute. MET stands for metabolic equivalent, and is the average amount of oxygen used by the body at a resting rate. There are three main factors that make up your total daily caloric expediture:
—60–70% accounts for resting metabolic rate
—10% accounts for food -digestion
—10–30% accounts for physical activity

Each individual has a different resting metabolic rate. Those who have a high resting metabolic rate hold an advantage in controlling their weight because they are able to burn more calories in a 24-hour period. There are many factors that affect our metabolic rate: age (adults half as fast as children); gender (males higher than females); exercise (raises met rate); very low calorie diets (lowers met rate); resistance exercise (lifting weights lifts the met rate); fever, catecholamines, thyroid hormones, testosterone, and growth hormones (raise the met rate).

PHYSICAL ACTIVITY AND ENERGY EXPENDITURE

Many people restrict their calories for weight loss and ignore physical activity. Physical activity contributes 20–30% to the body's total energy output. The number of calories needed for an activity depends exclusively on the muscles involved. The greater the amount of muscle mass used, the more effort used for intensity, and the longer duration of the activity—the more calories burned. Body size also plays a role on energy. The heavier the person, the more calories expended.

Activity	Kcal/hr.*	Time to Burn 250 Kcal
Rollerblading	345	45 Minutes
Walking or Tennis	400	35 Minutes
Swimming (45 yd./min.)	530	30 Minutes
Downhill Skiing	585	30 Minutes
Racquetball	600	25 Minutes
Jogging/Biking	650	25 Minutes
Running (7 mph)	850	17 Minutes
Cardio Kickboxing	900	17 Minutes
Example: Walking 30 min/day @ 210 cal. = 1 yr (76,650 cal.) = 22 lb. loss		

*(These figures are for a 150 lb. person. Add 10% for each 15 lbs. over 150; Subtract 10% for each 15 lbs. under 150.)

STRATEGIES FOR WEIGHT MANAGEMENT

Where do we begin? If our goal is to be healthy, and we want to work on weight management, we should try to accomplish this, by staying happy in the process. We must keep our self-confidence and motivation up. Accept who we are and go from there. We should take into consideration; our uniqueness, our life-style, and our physiology. We should strive to be knowledgeable and be responsible—we have a choice in our life to be more fit. Use your own values as a base. What works for you? What *will* you do, not what *should* you do. What is reasonable and practical, and what do we do most of the time? To be healthier and happier AND manage our weight, we MUST include exercise into our lives. Exercise is one of the most important factors in weight management. Activities should be consistent, regular and reasonable.

Fitness experts and exercise physiologists agree that a combination of aerobic exercise and weight training is most effective for reducing body fat. To burn excess fat deposits, longer workouts are more effective. When you begin your aerobic workout, carbohydrates are used as the main source of energy. Carbohydrates are quickly broken down and easily accessible to meet energy demands. During the first 20 minutes of aerobic exercise, carbohydrates are the primary energy supplier. Fat is broken down slowly and becomes the primary energy source after about 20 minutes of aerobics. The longer you work aerobically beyond 20 minutes, the more fat you utilize. Weight training is a vital component to increase lean body mass, basal metabolic rate, and burn more calories. Fat cannot be converted into muscle, but muscle can use fat energy to fuel its needs. Muscles burn more calories per hour at rest than fat cells.

Calories Burned Per Hour In Various Activities		Aerobic Miles Required To burn Off Snacks	
Golf	200	Beer 8 oz.	1.0
Walking 3 mph	275	Hamburger	2.0
Cycling 8 mph	330	French Fries	3.0
Rollerblading	400	Milk Shake	4.0
Racquetball	600	Chocolate Cake	4.2
Running 7 mph	850	Banana Split	6.2

F.I.T. FORMULA FOR MANAGING BODY COMPOSITION
AEROBIC WORKOUT TO DECREASE BODY FAT
F = 5–7 Days Per Week
I = 60–75% Maximum Heart Rate
T = Minimum of 30 Minutes
WEIGHT WORKOUT TO INCREASE LEAN BODY MASS
F = 3 Days Per Week
I = 60% 1 RM (10 Major Muscles)
T = Minimum of 30 Minutes

To control eating behaviors it is most often recommended that you keep a daily food diary or worksheet, as you did in Chapter 3. It is also important to note how you feel when you eat and what triggers your desire to eat. Many times we eat not for need of food or energy, but due to emotional stress or social pressure. Knowing what your behavior patterns are for eating, will help you start to change.

You must first make a mental commitment—set up goals and weight management strategies. What is realistic and attainable? How many calories should you consume daily? It varies depending on your age, sex, height, weight and activity level. Recommendations are:

	AGE	WEIGHT	HEIGHT	CALORIES PER DAY
MALES	19–50	160–175	5′10″	2,900
	51+	170	5′8″	2,300
FEMALES	19–50	128–138	5′5″	2,200
	50+	143	5′3″	1,900

It is recommended to reduce total caloric intake by 500 calories daily to lose 1# a week, but caloric intake should never go below 1,200/day.

Goals

- Lose 2 lbs. or less a week
- Maintain Balanced Meals
- Lose Body Fat, not Muscle
- Build Lean Body Mass (Muscle)
- Maintain Your Weight Loss
- Prevent a Slowing Metabolic Rate
- Eat sufficient Calories to Prevent Fatigue

First, you must reduce the amount of dietary fat you are consuming as well as the total number of calories . . . if your goal is to reduce weight or body fat. Second, you must cut down the amount of fat reserves you already have in your body. It is important to learn about reading labels. Products are deceiving . . . notice the percentage of calories of fat and especially, saturated fat.

Healthy eating and weight management go hand in hand. Consumed calories not utilized for energy demands—regardless of whether they come from carbohydrates, protein, or fat—are converted into fat and stored. You must be careful, when cutting down on calories. If you only reduce the amount of food you eat, you will decrease your Basal Metabolic Rate (BMR). This rate, as mentioned earlier, is the rate at which you burn calories. Exercise, keeps the BMR high during and after a workout. Remember, the *only* effective method to reduce weight and body fat is caloric and fat reduction, and exercise!

10 Tips to a Great Plate (Choosemyplate.gov)

Making food choices for a healthy lifestyle can be as simple as using these 10 Tips. Use the ideas in this list to balance your calories, to choose foods to eat more often, and to cut back on foods to eat less often.

1. **Balance Calories.** Find out how many calories YOU need for a day as a first step in managing your weight. Go to www.ChooseMyPlate.gov to find your calorie level. Being physically active also helps you balance calories.
2. **Enjoy Your Food But Eat Less.** Take the time to fully enjoy your food as you eat it. Eating too fast or when your attention is elsewhere may lead to eating too many calories. Pay attention to hung and fullness cues before, during, and after meals. Use them to recognize when to eat and when you've had enough.
3. **Avoid Oversized Portions.** Use a smaller plate, bowl, and glass. Portion out foods before you eat. When eating out, choose a smaller size option, share a dish, or take home part of your meal.
4. **Foods to Eat More Often.** Eat more vegetables, fruits, whole grains, and fat-free or 1% milk and dairy products. These foods have the nutrients you need for health—including potassium, calcium, vitamin D, and fiber. Make them the basis for meals and snacks.
5. **Make Half Your Plate Fruits and Vegetables.** Choose red, orange, and dark-green vegetables like tomatoes, sweet potatoes, and broccoli, along with other vegetables for your meals. Add fruit to meals as part of main or side dishes or as dessert.
6. **Switch to Fat-Free or Low-Fat (1%) Milk.** They have the same amount of calcium and other essential nutrients as whole milk, but fewer calories and less saturated fat.
7. **Make Half our Grains Whole Grains.** To eat more whole grains, substitute a whole-grain product for a refined product—such as eating whole-wheat bread instead of white bread or brown rice instead of white rice.
8. **Foods to Eat Less Often.** Cut back on foods high in solid fats, added sugars, and salt. They include cakes, cookies, ice cream, candies, sweetened drinks, pizza, and fatty meats like ribs, sausages, bacon, and hot dogs. Use these foods as occasional treats, not everyday foods.
9. **Compare Sodium in Foods.** Use the Nutrition Facts label to choose lower sodium versions of foods like soup, bread, and frozen meals. Select canned foods labeled "low sodium," "reduced sodium," or "no salt added."
10. **Drink Water Instead of Sugary Drinks.** Cut calories by drinking water or unsweetened beverages. Soda, energy drinks, and sports drinks are a major source of added sugar, and calories, in American diets.

HYPE? WHAT IS RIGHT?

Dr. Atkins' high protein diet was popular in 1972, and the *New Diet Revolution* became popular in 1991. Other best-selling books: *The Zone*, *Sugar Busters*, and *Protein Power* stress that many overweight people are carbohydrate sensitive . . . increased levels of sugar increases levels of insulin, and thus increases levels of stored fat.

The claim is that when one increases protein, it causes the body to burn its own fat. Similar to starvation, this produces ketone bodies that exceed the body's ability to remove them metabolically, a condition called **ketosis.**

Researchers are finding that it is not healthy to be in a prolonged state of ketosis. It causes nausea, vomiting, diarrhea, constipation, fatigue, bad breath and body odor. Some people call the high protein diet, the "stinky diet". When carbohydrates are restricted long term, our muscles aren't getting energy, and we feel tired, and fatigued. Some people have shown great success in a short time, but researchers find that after 6 months to a year, they are back at or over normal weight.

The Administrative Director at Duke University, Franca Alphin, R.D., in charge of the Diet and Fitness Center states, "The restrictions (of the high protein diet), will get you sooner or later—you are going to get bored and start craving the foods you can't have. You'll start to nibble, then before you know it, you'll be back to eating how you used to . . . and you won't have changed your eating habits or behavior." The healthy plan is one where you plan your meals, so you can change your bad eating habits.

POPULAR WEIGHT-LOSS METHODS DON'T PROMOTE BEHAVIOR CHANGE

Method	How It's Supposed to Work	Why It Doesn't
Diet Pills	Contain chemicals to suppress appetite or raise metabolic rate by stimulating the central nervous system.	Can cause high blood pressure dehydration & poor nutrient absorption. Dependency risk, > dosage need for same effect.
Special Food Combos	Certain food such as grapefruit burn fat. Special combinations fools your body into digesting them very differently, low absorption.	Not based on scientific fact. Limiting food choices will compromise nutrition. Unhealthy to maintain.
Liquid Meals or Packaged Foods	Control calories by replacing regular meals and snacks.	Products alone don't help you lose weight. Companies will package products w/low calorie diet & exercise plans.
Very Low Calorie <1,000 Cal/Day	Severe calorie restriction promotes faster weight loss.	May cause temporary loss of water weight, not long-term loss of fat. Tricks body into thinking it's starving. Body reacts by lowering calorie needs. They don't emphasize exercise & burning more cals.

Anorexia/Bulimia (Signs and Symptoms)

Many men and women with eating disorders appear NOT to be underweight. It does not mean they suffer less or are in any less danger. A sufferer does NOT need to appear underweight or even "average" to suffer any of these signs.

- Dramatic weight loss in a relatively short period of time.
- Wearing big or baggy clothes or dressing in layers to hide body shape.
- Obsession with weight and complaining of weight problems (even if thin).
- Obsession with calories and fat content of foods; reading books on disorders.
- Obsession with continuous exercise; preoccupied with food, weight, and cooking.
- Frequent trips to the bathroom immediately following meals (to vomit).
- Visible food restriction and self-starvation; keeping a food diary.
- Visible bingeing and/or purging; dizziness, headaches, hair loss; pale skin.
- Use or hiding of diet pills, laxatives, ipecac syrup (deadly), or enemas.
- Isolation. Fear of eating around and with others; low self-esteem.
- Unusual food rituals such as shifting the food around on a plate; cutting food into tiny pieces; using teeth to scrape food off the fork; not swallowing.
- Hiding food in strange places to avoid eating (anorexia) or to eat at a later time (bulimia).
- Flushing uneaten food down the toilet; complaints of feeling cold.
- Vague or secretive eating patterns; frequent sore throats/swollen glands.
- Low blood pressure; loss of menstrual cycle; constipation; insomnia.
- Perfectionist personality; mood swings; depression; fatigue; promiscuous.

Compulsive Overeating/Binge Eating Disorder (Signs and Symptoms)

A person suffering with binge eating disorder is at health risk for a heart attack, high blood-pressure and cholesterol, kidney disease and/or failure, arthritis and bone deterioration, and stroke.

- Fear of not being able to control eating; while eating not being able to stop.
- Isolation. Fear of eating around and with others.
- Chronic dieting on a variety of popular diet plans.
- Holding the belief that life will be better if she or he can lose weight.
- Hiding food in strange places to eat at a later time.
- Vague or secretive eating patterns.
- Self-defeating statements after food consumptions.
- Blaming failure in social and professional community on weight.
- Holding the belief that food is her or his only friend.
- Frequently out of breath after relatively light activities.
- Excessive sweating and shortness of breath; leg and joint pain; weight gain.
- High blood pressure and/or cholesterol; decreased mobility due to weight.
- Mood swings; depression; fatigue; insomnia; loss of sexual desire.

EXTREME APPROACHES TO WEIGHT LOSS

Spot reducing—is a fallacy which assumes that if you have fat deposits on your abdominals, exercising the muscles underlying that fat will make it go away. Fat is only burned through prolonged exercise (aerobically), and not from doing anaerobic, calisthenic exercises, like sit-ups. Fat is usually lost from top to bottom and is burned from all over the body, not one spot.

Surgery—is recently a popular method which some people resort to when all else fails. Surgery is not a cure for obesity nor a substitute for healthy eating and proper exercise. There are serious health problems which may occur from surgery. Lipo-suction has been performed since the early 1980's and though quickly removes fat from a specific area . . . is not a permanent or safe way to manage your weight.

Gastric Bypass: How It Works—Gastric bypass uses both a restrictive and a malabsorptive surgery technique. It restricts food intake and the amount of calories and nutrients the body absorbs. In addition to creating a smaller stomach pouch, the surgery changes the body's normal digestive process. As a result, food bypasses a large part of the stomach and most of the small intestine.

LAP-BAND: How It Works—Without any stomach cutting or stapling, the LAP-BAND® System reduces the stomach's capacity, restricting the amount of food one is able to eat at one time. Plus, the person feels full faster and stays full longer, thus eating less.

Fasting—is not recommended for people who want to lose weight. Fasting results in ketosis, a process in which the body first depletes its glycogen stores, then breaks down fat incompletely for energy. This incomplete breakdown of fat yields ketone bodies and this buildup in the blood can affect the body's natural acid-base balance. Extreme weakness and fatigue often accompany the loss of minerals and water. Metabolism slows and loss of fat falls to a minimum. Organs shrink and muscles atrophy, causing a reduction in energy needs.

Special Clothing and Wraps —are basically a quick fix, which is usually a loss of water weight. Perspiration leads to dehydration, again, water loss, not fat loss.

LEAN BODY MASS

Refer to Weight Management Worksheet

On your body composition lab sheet, find your pounds of Lean Body Mass (LBM), and your pounds of fat. Compare your Lean Body Mass with the chart below according to your sex and height.

	5'0	5'1	5'2	5'3	5'4	5'5	5'6	5'7
Women	70–86	73–89	75–91	78–93	81–96	83–99	86–102	90–105
Men						108–120	110–125	112–129
	5'8	**5'9**	**5'10**	**5'11**	**6'1**	**6'2**	**6'3**	**6'4**
Women	93–109	95–115	98–119					
Men	118–132	122–137	127–145	133–153	137–163	140–168	143–176	145–183

There are two basic methods of making your muscles harder and increasing your Lean Body Mass. First—lift weights with free weights or machines. Second—do muscle group work—calisthenics!

WORKSHEET 4 NAME ______________________________

Current Diet Programs

Describe three current **diets** being promoted on the market (not saunas, wraps, or exercise), and state the pros and cons of each.

DIET PROGRAM #1 Title:	PROS	CONS
DIET PROGRAM #2 Title:		
DIET PROGRAM #3 Title:		

(COMPLETE THE OTHER SIDE)

LEAN BODY MASS

Mary Jones	Age 43		
Height	5’5”		
Body Fat	30%	Pounds of Fat	________
Weight	130 Lbs.	Lean Body Mass	________

If Mary lost body fat down to 25%, yet weighed 138 pounds, this would result in an increased lean body mass of ________ pounds.

What **diet** suggestions would you make?

____

____

What type of **exercise** program would you suggest?

____

____

Sam Green	Age 20		
Height	6’2”		
Body Fat	17%	Pounds of Fat	________
Weight	185 Lbs.	Lean Body Mass	________

If sam lost body fat down to 12%, yet weighted 192 pounds, this would result in an increased lean body mass of ________ pounds.

A sensible program of **exercise** to gain Lean Body Mass should include:

____

____

Diet suggestions would be? ____

Precaution — to not use ____

BEHAVIOR MODIFICATION

Your Poor Eating Habits	Healthier Plan to Better Eating

Waist to Hip Ratio

PURPOSE: To determine your health risk from waist to hip ratio.

EQUIPMENT: Vinyl tape measure.

PROCEDURE: Measure the narrowest section of the bare waist as seen from the front while standing. Measure the hip girth at the largest circumference, which could be the hips, buttocks, or thighs, while standing. (*Do not compress* skin and fat with pressure from the tape).

FIGURE 4.1 Waist Girth

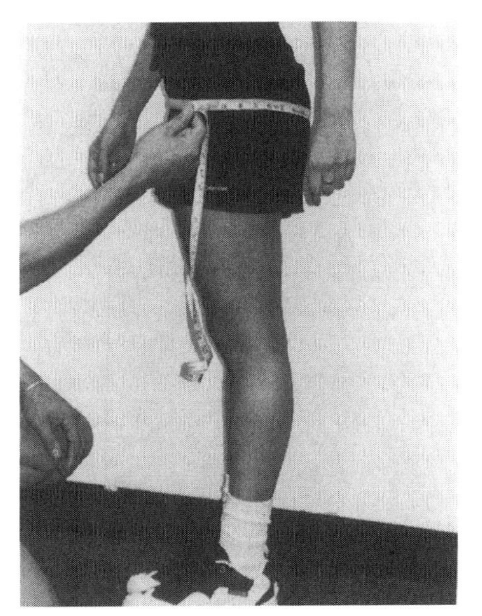

FIGURE 4.2 Hip Girth

WAIST MEASUREMENT______ DIVIDED BY HIP MEASUREMENT______

EX. __26__ ÷ __36__ = .72

YOURS ______ ÷ ______ = [ ]

WAIST: HIP RATIO ***** HEALTH RISK RATING SCALE			
RISK RATING	FITNESS CATEGORY	MEN	WOMEN
LOWER RISK	GOOD	<.95	<.80
Moderate Risk	Average	.96–1.0	.81–.85
Higher Risk	Poor	1.0+	.85+

WAIST TO HIP RATIO______________ FITNESS CATEGORY______________

LAB 2

Body Composition

SKINFOLD MEASUREMENT — WOMEN

PURPOSE: To estimate the percentage of body fat in women.

EQUIPMENT: Lange Skinfold Calipers
Body Composition measured by a fitness professional or use BMI Scale P. 73

PROCEDURE: Students will have three sites measured for the subcutaneous layer of fat.

Tricep ______________ mm

Suprailiac ______________ mm

Quadriceps ______________ mm

TOTAL SKINFOLDS Sum [ ]

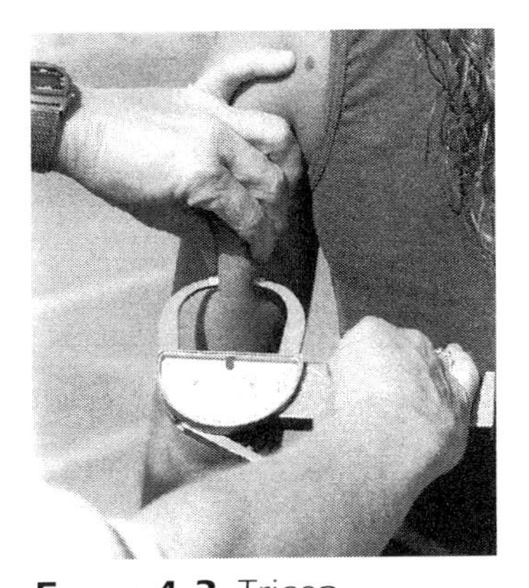

FIGURE 4.3 Tricep

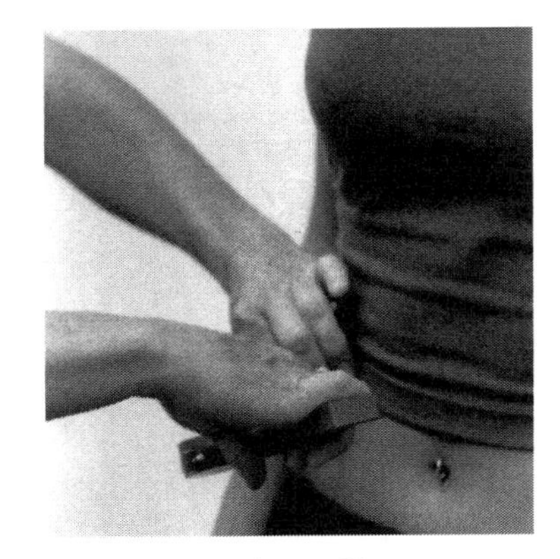

FIGURE 4.4 Suprailiac

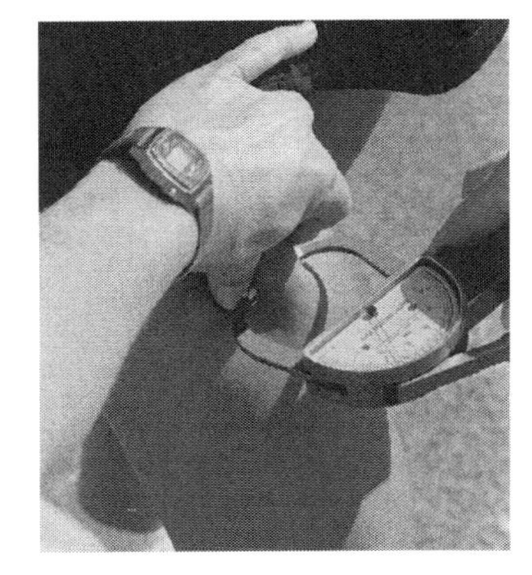

FIGURE 4.5 Quadriceps

BODY COMPOSITION CLASSIFICATION ACCORDING TO PERCENT BODY FAT					
Age	Excellent	Good	Average	Below Average	Poor
<29	<16%	17–19%	20–23%	24–27%	>27%
30–39	<17%	18–21%	22–25%	26–29%	>29%
40–49	<20%	21–24%	25–28%	29–32%	>32%
>50	<23%	24–27%	28–30%	31–35%	>35%

Source: Saddleback College

BODY FAT PERCENTAGE______________ FITNESS CATEGORY______________

TO FIND LEAN BODY MASS (LBM):

(Body weight × Body fat % = Lbs. of Fat)   *Body Wt. − # Fat = LBM*

(BW_______ × BF%_______ = _______# Fat)   BW_______ − _______ = _______

PERCENT FAT ESTIMATES FOR WOMEN									
	Age to the Last Year								
SUM OF 3 SKINFOLDS	UNDER 22	23 TO 27	28 TO 32	33 TO 37	38 TO 42	43 TO 47	48 TO 52	53 TO 57	OVER 58
23–25	9.7	9.9	10.2	10.4	10.7	10.9	11.2	11.4	11.7
26–28	11.0	11.2	11.5	11.7	12.0	12.3	12.5	12.7	13.0
29–31	12.3	12.5	12.8	13.0	13.3	13.5	13.8	14.0	14.3
32–34	13.6	13.8	14.0	14.3	14.5	14.8	15.0	15.3	15.5
35–37	14.8	15.0	15.3	15.5	15.8	16.0	16.3	16.5	16.8
38–40	16.0	16.3	16.5	16.7	17.0	17.2	17.5	17.7	18.0
41–43	17.2	17.4	17.7	17.9	18.2	18.4	18.7	18.9	19.2
44–46	18.3	18.6	18.8	19.1	19.3	19.6	19.8	20.1	20.3
47–49	19.5	19.7	20.0	20.2	20.5	20.7	21.0	21.2	21.5
50–52	20.6	20.8	21.1	21.3	21.6	21.8	22.1	22.3	22.6
53–55	21.7	21.9	22.1	22.4	22.6	22.9	23.1	23.4	23.6
56–58	22.7	23.0	23.2	23.4	23.7	23.9	24.2	24.4	24.7
59–61	23.7	24.0	24.2	24.5	24.7	25.0	25.2	25.5	25.7
62–64	24.7	25.0	25.2	25.5	25.7	26.0	26.2	26.4	26.7
65–67	25.7	25.9	26.2	26.4	26.7	26.9	27.2	27.4	27.7
68–70	26.6	26.9	27.1	27.4	27.6	27.9	28.1	28.4	28.6
71–73	27.5	27.8	28.0	28.3	28.5	28.8	29.0	29.3	29.5
74–76	28.4	28.7	28.9	29.2	29.4	29.7	29.9	30.2	30.4
77–79	29.3	29.5	29.8	30.0	30.3	30.5	30.8	31.0	31.3
80–82	30.1	30.4	30.6	30.9	31.1	31.4	31.6	31.9	32.1
83–85	30.9	31.2	31.4	31.7	31.9	32.2	32.4	32.7	32.9
86–88	31.7	32.0	32.2	32.5	32.7	32.9	33.2	33.4	33.7
89–91	32.5	32.7	33.0	33.2	33.5	33.7	33.9	34.2	34.4
92–94	33.2	33.4	33.7	33.4	34.2	34.4	34.7	34.9	35.2
95–97	33.9	34.1	34.4	34.6	34.4	35.1	35.4	35.6	35.9
98–100	34.6	34.8	35.1	35.3	35.5	35.8	36.0	36.3	36.5
101–103	35.2	35.2	35.7	35.9	36.2	36.4	36.7	36.9	37.2
104–106	35.8	36.1	36.3	36.6	36.8	37.1	3.3	37.5	37.8
107–109	36.4	36.7	36.9	37.1	37.4	37.6	37.9	38.1	38.4
110–112	37.0	37.2	37.5	37.7	38.0	38.2	38.5	38.7	38.9
113–115	37.5	37.8	38.0	38.2	38.5	38.7	39.0	39.2	39.5
116–118	38.0	38.3	38.5	38.8	39.0	39.3	39.5	39.7	40.0
119–121	38.5	38.7	39.0	39.2	39.5	39.7	40.0	40.2	40.5
122–124	39.0	39.2	39.4	39.7	39.9	40.2	40.4	40.7	40.9
125–127	39.4	39.6	39.9	40.1	40.4	40.6	40.9	41.1	41.4
128–130	39.8	40.0	40.3	40.5	40.8	41.0	41.1	41.5	41.8

The Cooper Institute for Aerobic Research, Dallas, Texas. Reprinted by permission.

LAB 2

Body Composition

SKINFOLD MEASUREMENT . .. MEN

PURPOSE: To estimate the percentage of body fat in men.

EQUIPMENT: Lange Skinfold Calipers
Body Composition measured by a fitness professional or use BMI Scale P. 73

PROCEDURE: Students will have three sites measured for the subcutaneous layer of fat.

Pectorals ____________ mm

Abdominals ____________ mm

Quadriceps ____________ mm

TOTAL SKINFOLDS Sum [ ]

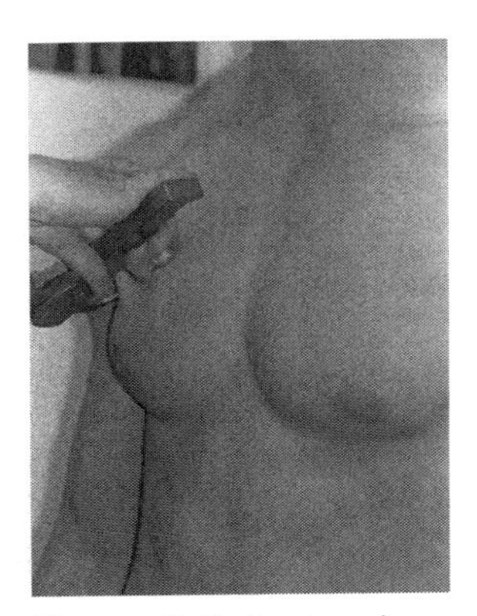

FIGURE 4.6 Pectorals

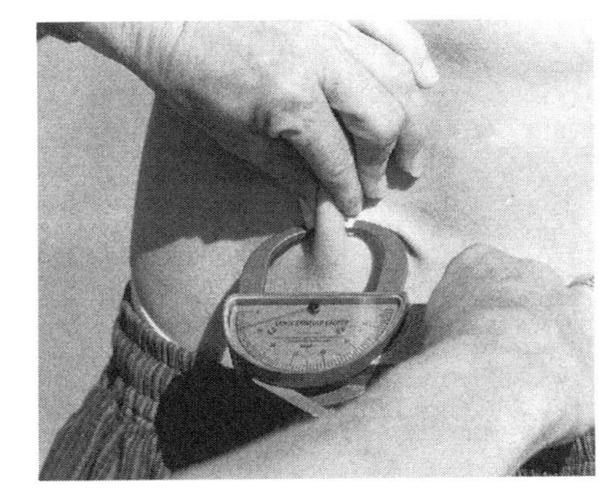

FIGURE 4.7 Abdominal

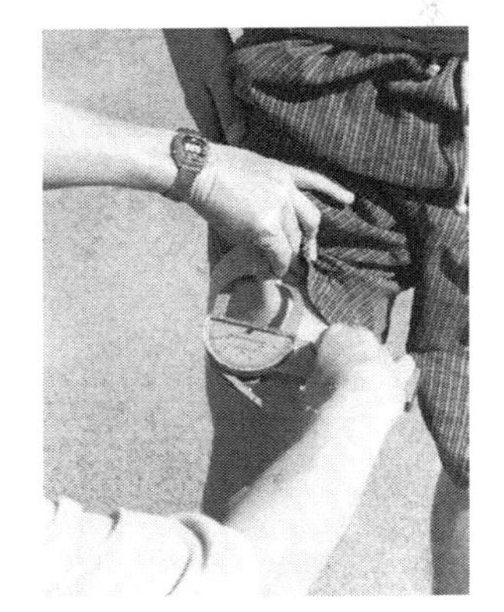

FIGURE 4.8 Quadriceps

BODY COMPOSITION CLASSIFICATION ACCORDING TO PERCENT BODY FAT					
Age	Excellent	Good	Average	Below Average	Poor
<29	<11%	12–15%	16–19%	20–23%	>23%
30–39	<15%	15–18%	19–21%	22–25%	>25%
40–49	<17%	18–21%	21–23%	24–27%	>27%
>50	<19%	20–22%	23–25%	25–28%	>28%

Source: Saddleback College

BODY FAT PERCENTAGE____________FITNESS CATEGORY____________

TO FIND LEAN BODY MASS (LBM):

(Body weight × Body fat % = Lbs. of Fat) Body Wt. – # Fat = LBM

(BW_______× BF%_______ = _______# Fat) BW_______–_______=_______

PERCENT FAT ESTIMATES FOR MEN (40 & UNDER)								
	Age to the Last Year							
SUM OF 3 SKINFOLDS	UNDER 19	20 TO 22	23 TO 25	26 TO 28	29 TO 31	32 TO 34	35 TO 37	38 TO 40
11–13	1.9	2.3	2.6	3.0	3.3	3.7	4.0	4.3
14–16	2.9	3.3	3.6	3.9	4.3	4.6	5.0	5.3
17–19	3.9	4.2	4.6	4.9	5.3	5.6	6.0	6.3
20–22	4.8	5.2	5.5	5.9	6.2	6.6	6.7	7.3
23–25	5.8	6.2	6.5	6.8	7.2	7.5	7.9	8.2
26–28	6.8	7.1	7.5	7.8	8.1	9.5	8.8	9.2
29–31	7.7	8.0	8.4	8.7	9.1	9.4	9.8	10.1
32–34	8.6	9.0	9.3	9.7	10.0	10.4	10.7	11.1
35–37	9.5	9.9	10.2	10.6	10.9	11.3	11.6	12.0
38–40	10.5	10.8	11.2	11.5	11.8	12.2	12.5	12.9
41–43	11.4	11.7	12.1	12.4	12.7	13.1	13.4	13.8
44–46	12.2	12.6	12.9	13.3	13.6	14.0	14.3	14.7
47–49	13.1	13.5	13.8	14.2	14.5	14.9	15.2	15.5
50–52	14.0	14.3	14.7	15.0	15.4	15.7	16.1	16.4
53–55	14.8	15.2	15.5	15.9	16.2	16.6	16.9	17.3
56–58	15.7	16.0	16.4	16.7	17.1	17.4	17.8	18.1
59–61	16.5	16.9	17.2	17.6	17.9	18.3	18.6	19.0
62–64	17.4	17.7	18.1	18.4	18.8	19.1	19.4	19.8
65–67	18.2	18.5	18.9	19.2	19.5	19.9	20.3	20.6
68–70	19.0	19.3	19.7	20.0	20.4	20.7	21.1	21.4
71–73	19.8	20.1	20.5	20.8	21.2	21.5	21.9	22.2
74–76	20.6	20.9	21.3	21.6	22.0	22.3	22.7	23.0
77–79	21.4	21.7	22.1	22.4	22.8	23.1	23.4	23.8
80–82	22.1	22.5	22.8	23.2	23.5	23.9	24.2	24.6
83–85	22.9	23.2	23.6	23.9	24.3	24.6	25.0	25.3
86–88	23.6	24.0	24.3	24.7	25.0	25.4	25.7	26.1
89–91	24.4	24.7	25.1	25.4	25.8	26.1	26.5	26.8
92–94	25.1	25.5	25.8	26.2	26.5	26.9	27.2	27.5
95–97	25.8	26.2	26.5	26.9	27.2	27.6	27.9	28.3
98–100	26.6	26.9	27.3	27.6	27.9	28.3	28.6	29.0
101–103	27.3	27.6	28.0	28.3	28.6	29.0	29.3	29.7
104–106	27.9	28.3	28.6	29.0	29.3	29.7	30.0	30.4
107–109	28.6	29.0	29.3	29.7	30.0	30.4	30.7	31.1
110–112	29.3	29.6	30.0	30.3	30.7	31.0	31.4	31.7
113–115	30.0	30.3	30.7	31.0	31.3	31.7	32.0	32.4
116–118	30.6	31.0	31.3	31.6	32.0	32.3	32.7	33.0
119–121	31.3	31.6	32.0	32.3	32.6	33.0	33.3	33.7
122–124	31.9	32.2	32.6	32.9	33.3	33.6	34.0	34.3

The Cooper Institute for Aerobic Research, Dallas, Texas. Reprinted by permission.

PERCENT FAT ESTIMATES FOR MEN (OVER 40)								
	Age to the Last Year							
SUM OF 3 SKINFOLDS	41 TO 43	44 TO 46	47 TO 49	50 TO 52	53 TO 55	56 TO 58	59 TO 61	OVER 62
11–13	4.7	5.0	5.4	5.7	6.1	6.4	6.8	7.1
14–16	5.7	6.0	6.4	6.7	7.1	7.4	7.8	8.1
17–19	6.7	7.0	7.4	7.7	8.2	8.4	8.7	9.1
20–22	7.6	8.0	8.3	8.7	9.0	9.4	9.7	10.1
23–25	8.6	8.9	9.3	9.6	10.0	10.3	10.7	11.0
26–28	9.5	9.9	10.2	10.6	10.9	11.3	11.6	12.0
29–31	10.5	10.8	11.2	11.5	11.9	12.2	12.6	12.9
32–34	11.4	11.8	12.1	12.4	12.8	13.1	13.5	13.8
35—37	12.3	12.7	13.0	13.4	13.7	14.1	14.4	14.8
38—40	13.2	13.6	13.9	14.3	14.6	15.0	15.3	15.7
41–43	14.1	14.5	14.8	15.2	15.5	15.9	16.2	16.6
44–46	15.0	15.4	15.7	16.1	16.4	16.8	17.1	17.5
47–49	15.9	16.2	16.6	16.9	17.3	17.6	18.0	18.3
50–52	16.3	17.1	17.5	17.8	18.2	18.5	18.8	19.2
53–55	17.6	18.0	18.3	18.7	19.0	19.4	19.7	20.1
56–58	18.5	18.8	19.2	19.5	19.9	20.2	20.6	20.9
59–61	19.3	19.7	20.0	20.4	20.7	21.0	21.4	21.7
62–64	20.1	20.5	20.8	21.2	21.5	21.9	22.2	22.6
65–67	21.0	21.3	21.7	22.0	22.4	22.7	23.0	23.4
68–70	21.8	22.1	22.5	22.8	23.2	23.5	23.9	24.2
71–73	22.6	22.9	23.3	23.6	24.0	24.3	24.7	25.0
74–76	23.4	23.7	24.1	24.4	24.8	25.1	25.4	25.8
77–79	24.1	24.5	24.8	25.2	25.5	25.9	26.2	26.6
80–82	24.9	25.3	25.6	26.0	26.3	26.6	27.0	27.3
83–85	25.7	26.0	26.4	26.7	27.1	27.4	27.8	28.1
86–88	26.4	26.8	27.1	27.5	27.8	28.2	28.5	28.9
89–91	27.2	27.5	27.9	28.2	28.6	28.9	29.2	29.6
92–94	27.9	28.2	28.6	28.9	29.3	29.6	30.0	30.3
95–97	28.6	29.0	29.3	29.7	30.0	30.4	30.7	31.1
98–100	29.3	29.7	30.0	30.4	30.7	31.1	31.4	31.8
101–103	30.0	30.4	30.7	31.1	31.4	31.8	32.1	32.5
104–106	30.7	31.1	31.4	31.8	32.1	32.5	32.8	33.2
107–109	31.4	31.8	32.1	32.4	32.8	33.1	33.4	33.8
110–112	32.1	32.4	32.8	33.1	33.5	33.8	34.2	34.5
113–115	32.7	33.1	33.4	33.8	34.1	34.5	34.8	35.2
116–118	33.4	33.7	34.1	34.4	34.8	35.1	35.5	35.8
119–121	34.0	34.4	34.7	35.1	35.4	35.8	36.1	36.5
122–124	34.7	35.0	35.4	35.7	36.1	36.4	36.7	37.1

The Cooper Institute for Aerobic Research, Dallas, Texas. Reprinted by permission.

Glossary of Terms

Adipose tissue is fat tissue.

Anorexia is a lack of appetite. Anorexia nervosa is a psychological and physiological condition characterized by inability or refusal to eat, leading to severe weight loss, malnutrition, hormone imbalances and other potentially life–threatening biological changes.

Body composition are the proportions of fat, muscle and bone making up the body. Usually expressed as percent of body fat and percent of lean body mass.

Bulimia, an eating disorder in which persistent overconcern with body weight and shape leads to repeated episodes of binging (consuming large amounts of food in a short time) associated with induced vomiting, use of laxatives, fasting, and/or excessive exercise to control weight.

Cellulite is a commercially created name for lumpy fat deposits. Actually this fat behaves no differently from other fat; it is just straining against irregular bands of connective tissue.

Fat-free weight is your lean body mass.

Ketosis is an elevated level of ketone bodies in the tissues. Seen in sufferers of starvation or diabetes, and a symptom brought on in dieters on very low carbohydrate diets.

Lean body mass (LBM) is the weight of the body, less the fat weight.

MET stands for "metabolic equivalent" and is defined as "the ratio of the work metabolic rate to the resting metabolic rate." One (1) MET is the rate at which adults burn kcal at rest: This is approximately 1 kcal per kilogram of body weight per hour (expressed as 1 kcal/kg/hr). Thus, the MET value of "sitting quietly and watching TV" is "1," whereas the MET value of "walking on level ground at moderate pace" is 3.3 (see table below). In other words, sitting quietly burns 1 kcal/kg/hr whereas walking on level ground at a moderate pace burns 3.3 kcal/kg/hr.

Metabolism is the total of all the chemical and physical processes by which the body builds and maintains itself and by which it breaks down its substances for the production of energy.

Obesity is excessive accumulation of body fat.

Spot reducing is an effort to reduce fat at one location on the body by concentrating exercise, manipulation, wraps, etc., on that location. Research indicates that any fat loss is generalized over the body.

Related Websites

Calorie Calculator
- www.coloriecounter.com
- www.nutritiondata.com

Nutri-System
- www.nutrisystem.com

Kids Weight
- www.kidsweight.com

Weight Watchers
- www.weightwatchers.com

Weight Loss
- www.eatright.org
- www.something-fishy.org
- www.ediets.com
- www.atkins.com
- www.southbeachdiets.com

Study Questions

Name ______________________________

1. What does the waist to hip measurement really indicate? Why is this important?

2. How many calories would *you* expend if you weighed 135 pounds and exercised for 30 minutes rollerblading? Walking? Jogging?

3. What would be one of the ideal strategies for weight management?

4. Which of the Eat Rights make Healthy Choices do *you* find to be the most difficult to follow?

5. What three (3) locations on the body are used to measure the fat for men and women with the skinfold method?

6. How many calories are available for energy in one pound of storage body fat?

7. What is the problem with using body weight on a scale to use as a goal? What would be a better measurement?

Muscle Strength and Muscle Endurance

KEY TERMS

Agonist	Isokinetic
Anabolic steroids	Isometric
Antagonist	Isotonic
Atrophy	Plyometric
Circuit training	Progressive resistance
Concentric	Repetition
Eccentric	Resistance
Extension	Set
Fast twitch	Slow twitch
Flexion	Strength
Hypertrophy	Testosterone

Muscle strength and endurance are components of physical fitness that affect almost every part of your daily life. Having sufficient strength to handle heavy objects periodically, i.e. moving furniture or trash cans, loading groceries to and from your car, or picking up babies or children are examples of your load carrying capacity. Being fatigued after a day's work could indicate a weakness in either of these two fitness components. You should have the energy to participate in some type of leisure time activity, maybe even active, at the end of the work day/week.

Usually there has been a narrow view of any form of strength training in the past, leaning toward the increased muscle mass of the body builder to a better performances in some type of athletic endeavor. While this is true, particularly in improved athletic performances, it is by no means the only gain from increased strength.

Other benefits of increasing your muscular strength and endurance could be in the assistance of managing your body fat. As shown in Chapter 4, a person will gradually lower their metabolism as they grow older. This also happens to people who are very sedentary and not physically active. Whether you slow down your metabolism from inactivity or aging, there is a tendency not to change the amount of calories you consume daily. If there was some way to increase the metabolism, in order to manage body fat, then many other problems associated with excess weight would be minimized or eliminated. Well, there is a way: become aerobically active *and* participate in strength training to increase your lean muscle mass which in turn increases your metabolism. This increase is not limited to just the exercise period but throughout the entire day. Body fat is almost entirely non calorie burning and lean body tissue is metabolically active and consuming many more calories, even at rest.

Another benefit from some form of strength training would be an improvement in your physical appearance. By cutting back on caloric intake, decreasing body fat, and increasing muscle mass and gaining muscle tone, your feelings of self worth should move up the positive scale. Emotionally, when you feel better about yourself and the way you look, this can transfer into a more self confident and self assured person.

TYPES OF MUSCLE

The human body has three different types of muscle tissue—a) *smooth* muscle tissue is involuntary and may be found in the digestive tract, walls of arteries, and iris of the eye; b) *cardiac* muscles (myocardium) are also involuntary and found only in the heart and create blood pressure by pumping blood in and out of the heart; and c) *skeletal* muscle fibers that voluntarily contract or pull the muscles that move bones of the skeleton and also are responsible for producing body heat. The references to muscle strength and/or endurance in this chapter will refer to the skeletal muscles.

Muscle Fibers

All skeletal muscles are comprised of two different types of smaller muscle fibers. These small fibers and their sub units of muscle tissue are either classified as **slow twitch** or **fast twitch.** How many do you have of each? One general nonscientific approach would be to go back to your childhood or some earlier time in your life and make comparisons with others that you may have played with in games or even formal competitions. All things being equal, i.e. training, size, age, skill level and strength, how did you compare?

Were you faster or quicker than most but would fatigue quickly, or did you move much slower but simply outlasted most of the competition. A higher percentage of fast twitch muscle fibers was probably the case in the first example whereas the second illustration would denote someone with more slow twitch fibers.

A more accurate, scientific and somewhat uncomfortable approach is to have a needle biopsy. Small amounts of muscle tissue are extracted, stained and observed under a microscope. Since the stained sample represents the whole muscle, a look at the ratio between fast twitch (since few capillaries are present in the fiber, it is sometimes called white) and slow twitch (many capillaries result in these fibers showing up red) would indicate your inherited trait. A high percentage of fast twitch fibers would show that since they are fast contracting, larger, but fatigue easier, they are best suited for short intense efforts. Weight lifters, sprinters and jumpers are examples of athletes that would have mostly fast twitch fibers. Conversely, a larger proportion of slow twitch muscle fibers, having a great blood supply and a slowness to fatigue, would likely result in a good performance in endurance activities as a long distance runner, cyclist or hiker.

The ratio of fast and slow twitch muscle fibers is determined by your parents. So if you wanted to become a world class athlete and excel in speed movements or long distance endurance, choose your parents wisely. Now training will have a great effect on how well these fibers perform. Present research shows that you cannot change a slow twitch fiber into a fast one and visa-versa. A person is able to improve their performance by either increasing the size of the muscle fibers called **hypertrophy** (primarily fast twitch) or developing a better oxygen carrying capacity of the slow twitch fibers.

Fiber Recruitment

Another consideration in the area of performance deals with the nerves that stimulate these fibers. The motor nerves, as opposed to sensory nerves, make the connection between the spinal cord and the muscle fibers. The number of fibers contacted by a motor nerve may be very large, due to numerous branches and may stimulate many fibers, such as the quadricep muscles in the leg or a small amount found in certain muscles of face or eyes. An unfit person may not be able to utilize many of their muscle fibers even for a maximum effort. Now this changes dramatically when a person goes through a strength-training program. Each of these motor units deals exclusively with a single type of muscle fiber, either fast or slow twitch. They do not intermix. The choice of which type of muscle fiber to recruit depends on the requirements of the activity and the muscles needed to perform that action. If a quick, explosive move like a jump is desired, then the fast twitch fibers would be utilized. However, if the activity would be of an endurance nature, as standing in a line or at attention, or a long run, then the slow twitch would be activated.

In trying to perform a quick muscle action repeatedly, like sprinting up stairs, there will be lactic acid accumulation, and fatigue will occur, making the explosive movement impossible to continue. Yet the body is still capable of using the slow twitch fibers of the same muscles, and although the reaction will be much slower, i.e. walking up the stairs, the muscles can still function.

MUSCLE STRENGTH

Muscular strength is the amount of force or weight that a muscle can exert or resist for a brief period of time. It is generally measured by a single maximal contraction of a muscle called a **1 RM**. Once the strength of a given muscle is known, then you can intelligently plan a program to improve or maintain it depending on your goals. Research and practical experience tell us that if we stress a muscle or muscle group more than it is normally accustomed to, it will eventually adapt and improve its function. Therefore, certain exercises can be designed to increase strength so that we may perform our everyday activities with less exertion and less chance of injury. If a muscle is stressed less than it is usually accustomed to, it will also adapt but it will atrophy and gradually lose strength. Persons who have had an arm or leg in a cast will notice the loss of muscle mass when the cast is removed. Use it or lose it!

Some things that result from inactivity or non weight bearing exercises (as shown by the early non exercising astronauts) would be 1) loss of muscle mass or lean body tissue, 2) loss of muscle strength or just getting weaker, 3) body fat may gradually increase (a popular term called 'creeping obesity'), and 4) decrease in optimal bone-mineral development possibly linked to osteoporosis.

MUSCLE ENDURANCE

In our present day society, it is necessary to have both muscular strength and endurance to function, yet muscular endurance depends on strength in order to be measured. Muscle endurance describes the ability of muscles to sustain repeated contractions (repetitions), *or* keep muscles under tension for an extended period of time. If having muscular strength allows you to pick up a heavy box once, then muscular endurance allows you to pick up ten boxes one after the other. Activities including sit ups, push ups, raking leaves, standing at attention, and applying pressure to a screwdriver or a wrench would all involve some type of localized muscle endurance. Once a person has sufficient strength to perform a series of repetitions, then improved performances will be dependent on muscular endurance training programs.

Quite often, women hesitate to participate in any form of resistance work, i.e. weight training, because of the fear of getting large, bulky muscles. Since women normally have a low level of male hormones, they are not likely to develop hypertrophy, unless they spend many hours a day for years in a weight lifting program. Firming muscles through weight training along with aerobics and diet management, may decrease the subcutaneous (area below the skin surface) fat and allow the muscles to begin showing.

As with any exercise program, there are certain principles you should know and understand in order to gain the maximum results from your efforts. If you have tried weight lifting before and were disappointed with the results or possibly injured through some omission of information or instruction, do not despair! While it is true that many people have the genetic makeup that will allow them to succeed quicker, apply all the principles to a sound weight training program and be the best that you can be.

Progression

One of the first things that a beginning exerciser, and in particular when training with weights, is to realize progress comes slowly. When the body is subjected to the physical stresses of exercise, it will either break down, (injury) from too much stress, or it will adapt to the load and show progress. However, if the demands on the muscles are reduced, such as in recovery from an illness or an injury, eventually there will be a loss of strength and muscle size. Even a long period of inactivity from a laid back vacation or changing to a sedentary lifestyle will cause the muscular system, (not the only system to be affected), to adapt and lose fitness.

Overload

Now that you are aware of adaptation to stress by the body, the next principle to consider is that of overload. Muscular development for either strength or endurance is dependent on the load or stress placed upon those muscles. In order to gain strength it will be necessary to add more resistance to those muscles than the amount they would normally receive in daily life. Overload can be systematically determined once you know what the level of strength is at the beginning of a weight training program. This is usually measured with a maximum amount of weight lifted one time after warming up with lighter weights. This is called a 1 repetition maximum (1 RM). Once you have your initial strength level, then gradually increase the amount or volume of work greater than what the muscle is accustomed to. This is the overload. As the muscle adapts to the increased load, then a new level of strength will be reached over time, another new 1 RM, and again a new overload. The plateaus shown on the graph (Figure 5.1) represent an unknown amount of time since there is no indication of the type of program being followed.

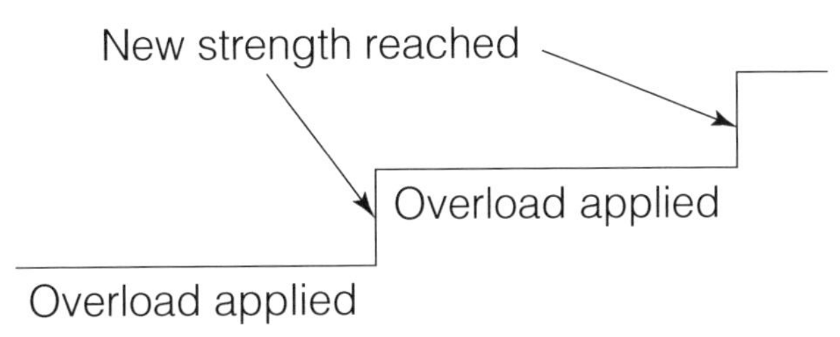

Figure 5.1 Overload and Body Adaptation

Progressive Resistance

The gradual increasing of resistance is sometimes known as progressive resistance training. Depending on the goal of your program, muscle strength or muscle endurance, the progressive overload principle would be varied to meet that objective. Usually when you want to gain specific muscle strength, the overload is a high percentage 80% + of your 1 RM, with repetitions less than 8–10. But you can also get an overload for strength by any one of the following:

- drop the number of reps (4–6) and raise the percentage
- increase the number of sets (4–8)
- increase the number of exercises for a specific muscle or group of muscles
- increase the number of workouts
- decrease the rest interval between sets

Again it is important to realize that all the options are not used at once, but only to vary the program and avoid boredom.

If muscle endurance was your goal then the same scenario would apply regarding overload. It would be advisable to obtain a measurement of your 1 RM on the muscles or groups of muscles that you wish to improve. Generally a lower percentage (50–70%) of your 1 RM is used with repetitions nearing 20 and 2 to 4 sets. The goal of overload can also be reached by

- increasing the total time of the workouts
- increasing the number of workouts
- decrease the rest period between sets.

It is important to remember that progression is dependent on active workout episodes, so if you apply too much stress (overload) on the body and it can't adapt, a breakdown occurs with a resultant loss of workout time. If this 'down time' is extensive, then you will lose much of what you have gained and have to backtrack to a new 1 RM and a new overload. Consistency in training is very important, since improvement is measured by a series of small steps leading up to the next goal.

Specificity

Another principle to understand is the term specificity. That was implied previously when referring to the general statements regarding the programs for increasing muscular strength or endurance. They are simply different programs of training. Your body will adapt to the stress imposed on it in a very specific manner. You get what you train for! If you want to develop strength then you will need to follow a program specific to that desired result but only for the muscles involved. Probably heavy weight with a few repetitions as the standard norm. But if muscle endurance is the goal then specifically let the muscles adapt to lighter weights and more repetitions. It would be unrealistic to expect increased strength by following a muscle endurance program. Yet many weight training beginners often are disillusioned for failing to follow the principle of specificity.

TYPES OF CONTRACTIONS

Your muscles contract or shorten under tension in 3 different ways. The three types of muscle contractions:

- Isotonic (movement)
- Isometric (no movement)
- Isokinetic (speed constant)

A training program may involve some of these approaches, but probably not all three. The principle of specificity would apply here since the goals and outcomes you desire would dictate certain techniques. The most common form of weight training would use isotonic contractions.

Isotonic Contraction

When the muscle contracts, thereby creating tension in the muscle, the result is movement and is called isotonic. During this type of workout motion, it is important to emphasize the use of both phases for maximum results. The **concentric** phase occurs when the muscle length is shortening by overcoming the resistance and moving through its range of motion or ROM for that muscle. An **eccentric** contraction happens when that same muscle is now lengthened, under tension, as it is returned to the starting position.

An example of these two phases in action is shown in the movement of the bicep (arm) curl. This lift is often used to increase the size of the upper arm. The bicep muscle, attached to the front of the upper arm, is shortened as it pulls the resistance through the arms' full ROM for half the repetition. Rather than just letting gravity drop the weight back down, you lower the weight under tension, returning the bicep muscle to its original length. This technique of concentric (positive) and eccentric (negative) contractions will give you the maximum results. Concentric is always going to be a pulling or pushing action of the muscle, while eccentric usually opposed the effect of gravity by resisting or opposing it. (See Figure 5.2.)

Isometric Contraction

Any lift when the muscles contract creating tension yet does not result in any movement is an isometric contraction. There is no shortening of the muscle which should occur when you are lifting a weight and find that you no longer can move that resistance because fatigue has set in and you may

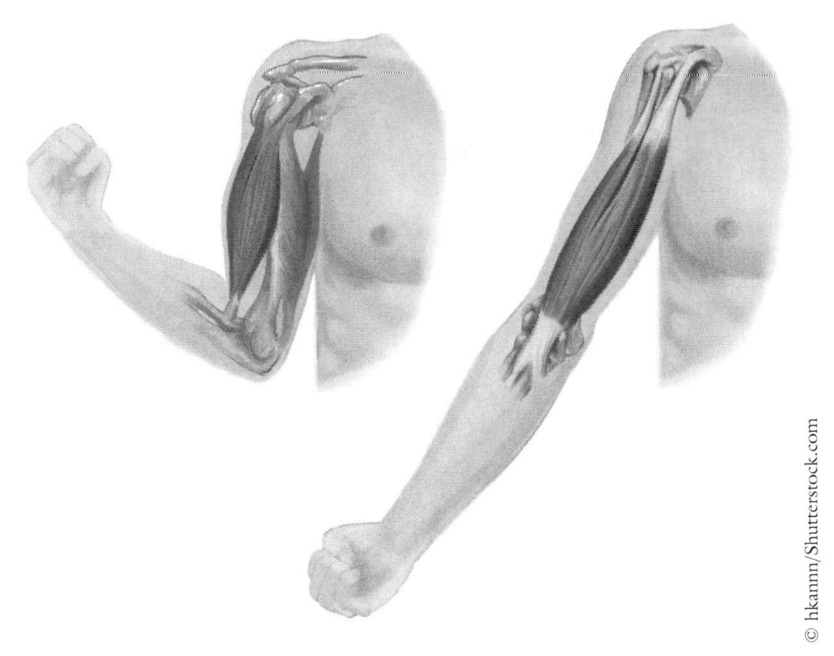

FIGURE 5.2 Bicep Muscle Contraction

require help to safely lower the weight. One of the purposes of a spotter when using free weights is to provide that help.

Early in the 1950's, a couple of German researchers (Hettinger and Mueller) stated that a short isometric workout on a daily basis would develop muscular strength. By spending approximately 6–10 seconds for a few attempts (2–5) at a nearly maximum contraction trying to move something that won't move, strength would result. In the 50's and even into the 60's, isometric contraction as a new means of acquiring strength virtually swept the country, from professionals down to the high schools. Everyone was huffing and puffing trying to move some immovable object, i.e. walls, doorways, weights, or opposing limbs of the body all hoping for 'instant' strength.

However, further research revealed some inherent disadvantages to this approach. Strength that is gained is specific only to the angle of the joint in which the contraction was held. Since nothing is going to move, there would be no way to measure the intensity of your effort, simply your assurance that it was nearly a maximal effort. Because the muscles are not going through contraction of squeezing and relaxing, the flow of blood is reduced and yet the intensity would be high with a gain in blood pressure (may be serious for people having hypertension). Primarily used now to help rehabilitate an injured muscle.

Isokinetic Contraction

An isokinetic contraction is the third type, which is similar to isotonic, except the speed is constant and the resistance changes as the muscles move through their ROM. Since a muscle is able to handle more resistance during its range due to a better angle of leverage at the joint, isokinetic machines are designed to deliver this resistance. Now the manner in which the muscles work is different than an isotonic contraction. In that contraction, a single muscle or group of them would contract concentrically to its limit and then an eccentric contraction would take place for the same muscle(s) back to the beginning position. With isokinetics, a muscle or group would contract concentrically with ever increasing resistance to its limit and then the opposite muscle or group would

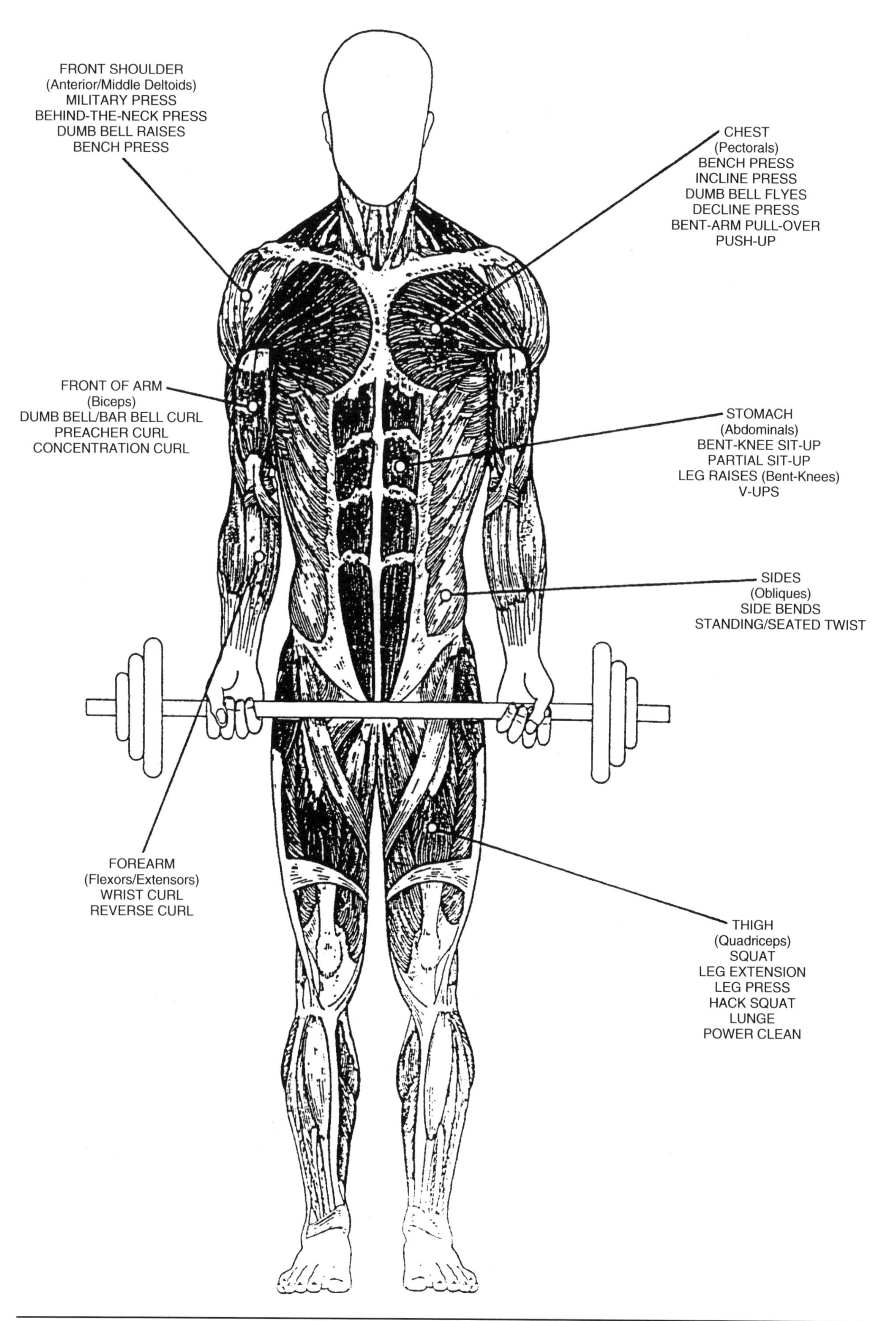
FRONT SHOULDER
(Anterior/Middle Deltoids)
MILITARY PRESS
BEHIND-THE-NECK PRESS
DUMB BELL RAISES
BENCH PRESS
CHEST
(Pectorals)
BENCH PRESS
INCLINE PRESS
DUMB BELL FLYES
DECLINE PRESS
BENT-ARM PULL-OVER
PUSH-UP
FRONT OF ARM
(Biceps)
DUMB BELL/BAR BELL CURL
PREACHER CURL
CONCENTRATION CURL
STOMACH
(Abdominals)
BENT-KNEE SIT-UP
PARTIAL SIT-UP
LEG RAISES (Bent-Knees)
V-UPS
SIDES
(Obliques)
SIDE BENDS
STANDING/SEATED TWIST
FOREARM
(Flexors/Extensors)
WRIST CURL
REVERSE CURL
THIGH
(Quadriceps)
SQUAT
LEG EXTENSION
LEG PRESS
HACK SQUAT
LUNGE
POWER CLEAN

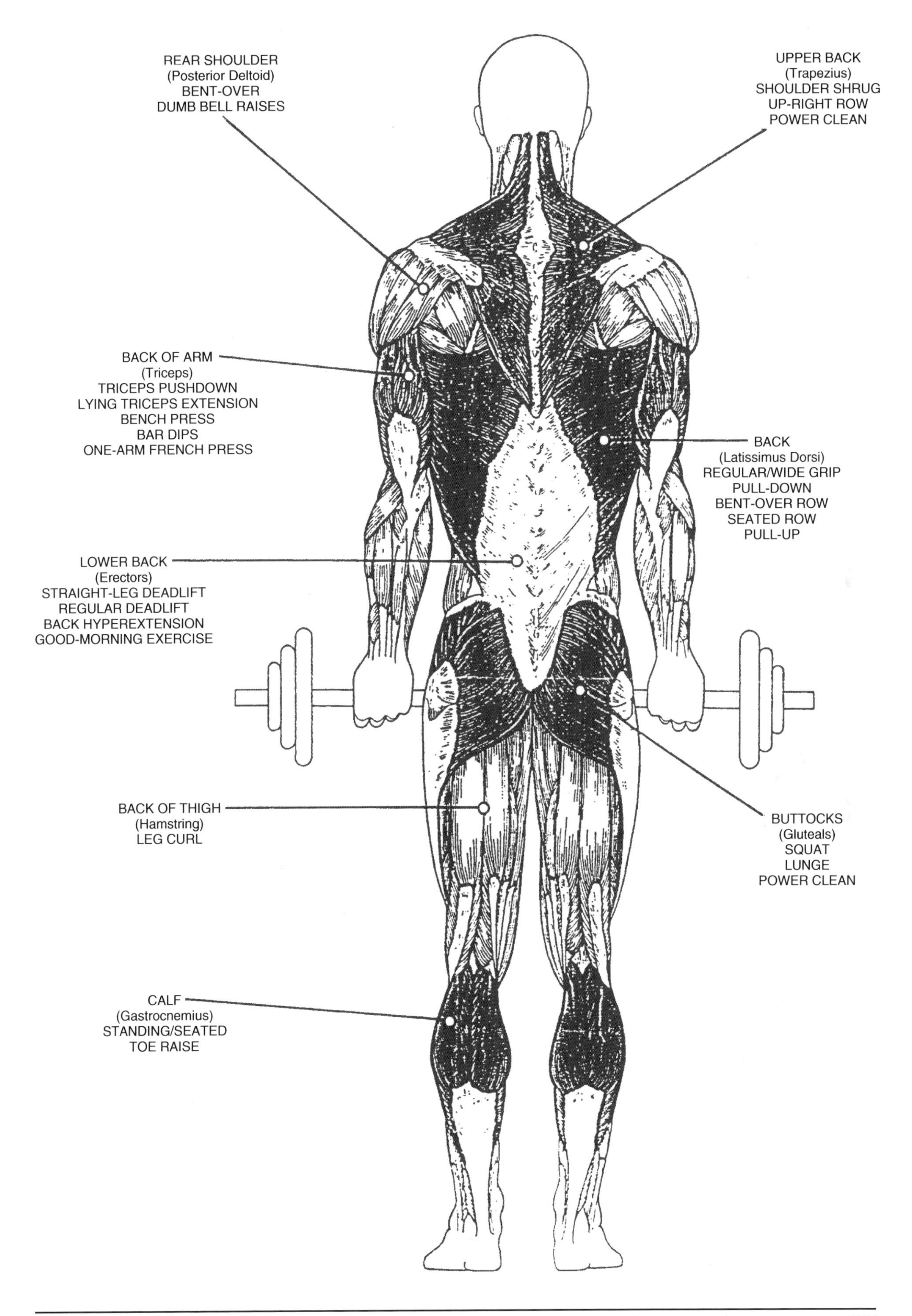
REAR SHOULDER
(Posterior Deltoid)
BENT-OVER
DUMB BELL RAISES
UPPER BACK
(Trapezius)
SHOULDER SHRUG
UP-RIGHT ROW
POWER CLEAN
BACK OF ARM
(Triceps)
TRICEPS PUSHDOWN
LYING TRICEPS EXTENSION
BENCH PRESS
BAR DIPS
ONE-ARM FRENCH PRESS
BACK
(Latissimus Dorsi)
REGULAR/WIDE GRIP
PULL-DOWN
BENT-OVER ROW
SEATED ROW
PULL-UP
LOWER BACK
(Erectors)
STRAIGHT-LEG DEADLIFT
REGULAR DEADLIFT
BACK HYPEREXTENSION
GOOD-MORNING EXERCISE
BACK OF THIGH
(Hamstring)
LEG CURL
BUTTOCKS
(Gluteals)
SQUAT
LUNGE
POWER CLEAN
CALF
(Gastrocnemius)
STANDING/SEATED
TOE RAISE

also contract concentrically until back to the original starting position. So in one lifting movement, you have exercised two opposing muscles to their maximum reducing the usual time needed to work out.

Muscle Imbalance

Often individuals have sufficient strength in some muscle groups but are deficient in others, a muscular imbalance. This is particularly evident when comparing the relative strength of the quadriceps (muscles in front of the thigh) and the opposing muscle group called the hamstrings (muscles in back of the thigh). The quads are in constant use every time we walk, run, climb stairs, or jump, while the hamstrings don't receive the necessary amount of stimulation doing these same activities to maintain equal balance. This type of muscular imbalance, with the quads pulling with more force than the weaker hamstrings, is often the source of running injuries to the rear thigh. Another more common example of muscular imbalance could be found in the problem of a sore lower back. Since there are many adults (80%) in the American society that can lay claim to having had low back trouble in their lives, interest in prevention is certainly there. Occasionally, this may be orthopedic and need medical intervention. But many lower back problems may be a result of muscle imbalance between the abdominals (weak and/or stretched), and the lower back (stronger but tight) and often compounded by the weak tight hamstrings (See Figure 5.3). When using strength training to improve health, it is important to concentrate on the weaker muscles to create a balance. A good rule is to remember: STRETCH THE STRONG MUSCLES AND STRENGTHEN THE WEAK ONES!

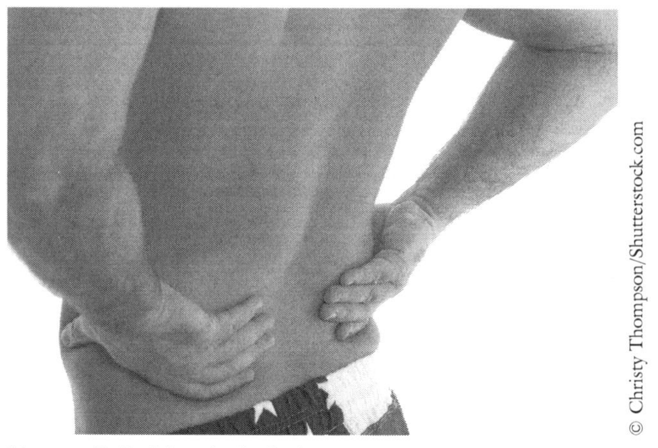

FIGURE 5.3 Muscle Imbalance

When a group of muscles working together contract, causing a movement around a joint, then they are classified as **agonists**, i.e. bending the elbow by contracting the bicep muscle to create flexion. However, if a muscle that is opposite this muscle contracts afterward, then they are the **antagonists** creating a different action, i.e. straightening the elbow by contracting the tricep muscle with the result—extension. If muscles that contract are in opposition to another set of muscles when they contract, then they are called antagonistic pairs (Table 5.1). For a movement to function normally, i.e. walk, bend your arm, bend over, throw a ball or hit a ball then the antagonistic pairs of muscles have to work in harmony. When one muscle contracts then its opposite must relax allowing the bones to move. If both contracted there would be no movement just an isometric contraction. In any athletic performance, this interchange of nerve stimulation and muscle reaction are very complex and in a constant state of change as the activity continues.

- Front of the arm (Biceps)—Back of the arm (Triceps)
- Chest (Pectorals)—Upper back (Trapezius)
  Mid back (Latissimus Dorsi)
- Stomach (Abdominals)—Lower back (Erector Spinae)
- Buttocks (Gluteals)—Hip Flexors
- Front of the thigh (Quadriceps)—Back of thigh (Hamstrings)
- Front of lower leg (Tibialis Anterior)—Calf (Gastrocnemius)

Table 5.1 Examples of Opposing or Antagonistic Muscle Groups

Another pair of movements of the skeletal system, in addition to flexion and extension, would be abduction and adduction. Abduction is any movement away from the center of the body. Conversely, adduction is any movement toward the mid line of the body. If a person raises an arm or leg outwardly from the body, this is abduction. Bringing the arm or leg back to the starting position would be classified as adduction.

WEIGHT TRAINING PROGRAMS

Before embarking on a weight training program, either by yourself, joining a fitness center or even enrolling in a class, you should make some mental inquiries. What are your goals and what do you hope to gain? Be as specific as possible so any advice you receive can be integrated or rejected in the planning stages. You do not have to be limited to only one goal. Many goals can and often are compatible with each other and may even change as your knowledge and program develop. Set short term goals as well as long and far reaching goals. Give yourself a realistic timetable in order to achieve these objectives and yet be flexible enough to adapt to the inevitable interruptions that occur. Examples of some weight training goals are in Table 5.2.

- Develop overall strength of the body
- Develop strength for a specific athletic performance
- Develop strength in the rehabilitation of a muscle
- Develop muscular endurance
- Build more lean body mass and reduce fat
- Develop overall muscle tone and look better
- Develop more power for specific athletic performances

Table 5.2 Examples of Various Goals

The bottom line, regardless of the goals and timeline you set for yourself in the beginning, is how much do you want it? What is the motivation and how long can you keep the 'inner fires burning'? Imagine what you will represent to yourself (self concept) and others upon reaching that goal. How will you look different?

RESISTANCE EQUIPMENT

An overview of the types of equipment that may be available to you and some of the advantages and disadvantages of each.

An isotonic contraction is usually performed on equipment that falls into either one of two different types. The first is called fixed resistance, i.e. free weights (dumbbells, barbells), your own body weight (calisthenics) and some weight machines. This means that the resistance doesn't change regardless of which muscles are used. A 20 lb. dumbbell will stay at 20 lbs even if it is moved fast or slow. There is more tension built up in the muscle at the beginning of the lift where you are the weakest of the total ROM. So with fixed resistance equipment, the part of the muscle that has the least amount of strength will be getting the most overload and gradually decrease depending on the amount of leverage.

The other type of equipment used in isotonic contraction is a variable resistance machine. The advantage of this approach is related to the construction of the machine emphasizing quick weight changes and safety, since a spotter is not necessary. By changing the resistance and allowing it to increase, as the muscle travels through its ROM, it causes a higher overload on the muscles than with fixed resistance. Since it is an isotonic contraction, both the concentric and eccentric phases of the movement are still an important factor for complete development.

Weakest Point Principle

An example of a characteristic of strength development deals with gaining maximum strength at the weakest point in the range of a specific joint. Regarding the bicep curl lift (see Figure 5.4), it helps to understand that as the arm moves from straight down to a flexed arm position the amount of tension created in the bicep muscle varies. Because the length of the arm and the angle of the elbow joint changes from a weak position (straight down) with the levers (upper and lower arm) all lined up to

the strongest angle as it approaches a flexed bicep. Continuing the movement on up to a fully flexed curl reduces the tension, but not as weak as at the beginning. So, if you are training with a fixed resistance, the muscle has the highest overload at the start of the lift (weakest position) and would benefit the most near the beginning. Since the weight won't change, (fixed) the muscle would not receive as much overload, and yet would still gain some strength. It is important to guard against taking advantage of the momentum created as you move the weight toward a stronger position and negating some of the overload.

Again, with fixed resistance equipment, you will be doing isotonic work involving a concentric contraction and eccentric contraction. With the negative work, you can experience more muscle soreness or possible injury. In particular, a spotter is desirable, and certainly necessary if using barbells with heavy weights or when fatigued. It does limit some types of strength training programs from the point of view regarding safety, specially when working out alone. This situation may occur frequently when a person has a garage or room full of weights and no workout partner. There is also the expense of purchasing fixed resistance equipment for the home or the cost of joining a fitness facility.

Some of the advantages of performing isotonic work on this equipment would be a feeling of success because you can measure your intensity and can document where you started and your progress. This process can be motivational, since you are constantly receiving feedback on the program you selected. It is easy to adjust the workouts as the body adapts to the overload after the plateau period and a new intensity can be applied. The result will be added strength throughout the ROM due to that overload. If your goal is to increase muscle size (hypertrophy), it is easy to accomplish with this equipment, along with the ability of working the major muscles of the body.

© Diego Cervo/Shutterstock.com

Variable Resistance

The variable resistance equipment used in an isotonic contraction will bring about many of the same advantages with fixed resistance. But because the resistance can be changed, there is a greater amount of tension created in the muscles as it progresses through the range of motion. This would allow for even greater strength gains in the muscle overall, yet the weakest point will be overloaded the most. The ease of adjusting the weight selection faster would be an added benefit reducing the total workout time. Since changing the locking selector pins is done quite easily, there is a definite advantage in the safety features of these types of machines.

Accommodating Resistance

When comparisons are made regarding the use of accommodating resistance, the transition to isokinetic contraction exercises is usually the mode. In the use of accommodating resistance machines, the tension or force created by the person lifting is equaled with a similar amount of resistance by the machine. So, regardless of the speed used, the resistance of each (lifter and machine) will be equalled throughout the ROM. The lifting movement will utilize only concentric contractions, or positive pressure, but involving two different opposing muscles. One muscle group may push the resistance one direction and then an opposing muscle group may pull the resistance back to the beginning, both concentric moves. There is no eccentric contraction in an accommodating machine utilizing an isokinetic lift resulting in little, if any, soreness.

If the opportunity would arise in choosing what type of equipment is best for you, fixed weight, variable resistance, or accommodating resistance, there is one common workout thread of training. What matters the most, is the quality of your workouts, not the type of equipment you use. The total amount of work you perform is the bottom line for development.

SPECIAL STRENGTH TRAINING PROGRAMS

Plyometrics

Some of the programs that are skill related emphasize the technique to gain an edge on the competition through certain training methods. One example of such a program is **plyometrics**. A plyometric exercise involves a sudden eccentric stretching action of the muscles followed by a forceful concentric contraction of those same muscles. A favorite drill to increase the jumping ability of the legs is to jump forward from a box down to the ground and then to rebound up onto another box. This type of training, if not done to excess, can provide sufficient overload to increase leg strength, or more specifically because speed is added, the explosive power of the legs. Depending on the sport and strength of the athlete, various forms of plyometrics can improve any vertical jumping capacity for basketball, volleyball, track and field, or football. Each training program can be altered to fit the specific skill needed, i.e. a single vertical jump or repetitions (basketball, volleyball) and a single horizontal jump or repetitions (long and triple jump) (see Table 5.3). This training technique can be used for the upper body as well in the arms and shoulders, or back. Catching a medicine ball and then quickly throwing it back would preload the above muscles and a concentric contraction to follow. Care should be taken not to overuse this type of training.

▪ Knee Lifts—Gradually lift feet higher & faster	(5 Minutes)
▪ Single Leg Hops—1 Leg hop, land on both feet	(10 × Each)
▪ Power Jumps—Straight up, knees high as possible	(10 ×)
▪ Bounds—Standing long/high jump	(10 ×)
▪ Lateral Jumps—Same except sideways	(5 × Each Way)
▪ Walking Lunges—Low position	(100 Yards)

Table 5.3 Samples of Plyometric Exercises

Periodization

Periodization of training is a technique used mostly by highly trained competitive athletes. Training with this method involves the changing of the intensity of the workload to create, usually four or more different yet specific results. The purpose is to reach a maximum or peak performance at a specific time or event in the future. By adjusting the workload periodically during the year, the athlete should note the effects on the body as adaptation occurs. This will be of benefit on the altering of various training programs. Since there is changing of a goal with each specific period, not a single method is run into the ground reducing the chance of boredom and overtraining. Some periods might emphasize general conditioning, i.e. preseason, but another period might require a need to gain maximum strength (off season) or simply maintenance (in season). A good example of periodization at work with an elite athlete would be the preparation for the Olympics or similar type of world championship.

The average person can also use this method to vary the intensity in a weekly or bi-weekly program. Instead of repeating the same lift for each workout, substitute a new lift but still working the same muscle area. Incline/decline in place of a flat bench press; bench dips for bar dips; shoulder shrugs or bent over rows for shoulder press and upright row.

TYPICAL TRAINING SYSTEMS

The following systems or methods of training will usually apply to any of the equipment explained before. They are simply variations of different techniques that may be applied to your basic routine. Stay with a fundamental approach that you will be happy with or explore with some other techniques to find an alternate routine. These other options can be for a change of pace from the norm to use for measurement or just to avoid boredom.

There are some basic terms to become familiar with so you will be able to determine the value of different systems and their application to meet your goals.

Repetitions or reps are the number of times you repeat the lift without rest and with the same weight selection.

Sets are a group of repetitions performed in a single attempt. The amount of rest between sets is determined by the specific goal.

Resistance is a given load or weight that is applied against a muscle during a single exercise. Sometimes this is expressed as a percentage of your strength for that lift as opposed to a specific weight.

One Repetition Max

One method of determining the amount of resistance to be used in a lifting routine is to find out how strong you are with a one repetition maximum or a 1 RM. The amount of weight lifted represents the most resistance that can be moved one time (rep) during a specific lift. By starting with a low weight (something that you will not have any difficulty) and then adding more weight after each successful repetition. You will gradually work your way up to a maximum effort. Hopefully, you will be able to accomplish this maximum weight without fatigue becoming a factor, usually by the 5th attempt. (Note Lab 3 for strength.)

There are other variations on the 1 RM (which represents your strength or the most you can lift one time) approach. Some systems use a 10 RM, or the highest weight you can lift no more than 10 repetitions. The concept is the same in both cases since you will be working out with a fraction of your strength, just different systems to reach distance goals (principle of specificity).

Rest or recovery between sets is the amount of time that usually determines the type of goal desired. Usually more rest is given for strength or muscle size (hypertrophy) program, since the intensity of the sets is relatively high. The more endurance or toning desired as a goal reduces the amount of rest since the intensity or amount of resistance is lowered but the repetitions are extended.

Frequency of weight training workouts usually is limited to 3 days a week or a minimum of 48 hours of recovery from the previous workout using the same muscles. Occasionally, athletes or very dedicated lifters utilize a workout 4 days a week, doing a split routine, using different muscle groups on back to back days but not repeating those same muscles until they have recovered 48 hours.

Pyramid

One training system involves a technique called a **pyramid**, primarily used for gaining strength. Sometimes called a light to heavy system, which really describes the routine. Starting with a light weight and gradually progressing to a heavy weight, you have built in a warmup and then working your way up until reaching an overload. Delorme introduced this technique during the 50's using the following formula:

1 set 10 reps @ 50% of 10 RM
1 set 10 reps @ 75% of 10 RM
1 set 10 reps @ 100% of 10 RM

One disadvantage of this method is a certain amount of fatigue from the earlier efforts that may compromise the ability to easily succeed with the third set at maximum overload. A variation of this system utilizes a decrease in the reps as the resistance increases for each set, sometimes with intermediate weights and increasing the sets to 4 or 5. Mainly designed for strength.

Another system involves the pyramid except in inverse order with the heavy weight first when you are not fatigued. A proper warmup is essential first since you are starting with a maximum effort, hopefully not with cold muscles. After the initial heavy lift, you then reduce the resistance but keeping the reps constant, or possibly decreasing the weight and also decreasing the reps. This workout schedule would be like this:

1 set of 10 @ 90–100% 1 RM
1 set of 10 @ 70– 80% 1 RM
1 set of 10 @ 50– 60% 1 RM

-or-

1 set of 10 reps @ 90–100% 1 RM
1 set of 8 reps @ 70– 80% 1 RM
1 set of 6 reps @ 60– 70% 1 RM
1 set of 4 reps @ 50– 60% 1 RM

It is even possible to combine the two pyramid techniques in one workout, i.e. light to heavy and then heavy to light. Experiment with the number of reps to experience a safe maximum overload for muscle strength or hypertrophy.

One Set to Failure

Another system is called a failure or 1 set to failure. The concept is to overload the muscles to the maximum by lifting a weight, usually in a slower, more deliberate manner, and from 10 to 15 reps. This resistance will create a failure in those muscles approaching the last rep. Accomplishing only one set in this method insures that the muscle involved has been totally overloaded and can do no more work. A shorter workout time is another advantage.

A similar technique uses the heavy to light weight approach with a specific weight and a given number of reps then without resting you reduce the weight and do as many reps as possible. This continues down to a light weight but a totally fatigued muscle. Definite accumulation of lactic acid in the muscles resulting in a 'burn' or tightness.

Set System

The set system has a few variables. Many people that start out lifting weights have used the constant set system, represented by a fixed weight and a certain number of reps, i.e. 3 sets of 10 reps @ 60 lbs. This method is often used when the technique of measuring your strength was with a 1 or 10 RM. Some experts have stated that you should have difficulty with the last few reps in each set for strength development. The same approach can be altered slightly, with a lighter weight and more repetitions with the desired goal of muscle toning or endurance.

Super Set

Set variation two is classified as a **Super Set**. This technique involves two exercises in succession without resting between the sets. The muscles in action are antagonistic or opposite to each other. While in exercise one, the bicep muscle is the agonist or prime mover in a curl or flexion movement with the triceps (antagonist) resting. Then without any rest you switch to a tricep extension while the bicep is recovering. The amount of resistance would vary according to the strength of the muscles involved. This routine of 2 sets in a row with 10 reps each and then a rest may be repeated two or three times until the muscles are exhausted.

Circuit Training

Another system that is used, usually with some type of machine because of the ease of weight selection, no need for a spotter, and the speed with which you make changes going from one machine to another. This is **Circuit Training**, and it is an advantage when large numbers of people are working out or you wish to get a total body workout in a relatively short period of time. An antagonistic circuit is set up working opposing muscle groups back to back. When the first set of muscles is partially recovering from its work, the opposite muscle is now going through its own contractions, and so on using different pairs of muscles in succeeding exercises. By repeating the exercises, somewhere between 10 to 20 stations in each circuit, and using approximately 50% of their 1 RM for a fixed period of time, i.e. 30–45 seconds, you will accomplish an overload as fatigue sets in. Usually a great cardiorespiratory workout, especially if you add an aerobic activity between every station for a similar time of 30–45 seconds. The aerobic activity may vary between a mini trampoline, stair stepping, stationary bicycle, walking or jogging around, all designed to maintain your heart rate in the aerobic training zone. This system primarily leads to muscle endurance and toning with any strength occurring as your muscles become overloaded due to the number of circuits completed (see Figure 5.4). That method is also known as the Super Circuit. A calisthenic type circuit can be incorporated by doing a combination of push ups, jumping jacks, abdominal work, pull ups, side bends, hopping, stair stepping, or jumping rope all for a specific time or number of reps.

SAFETY CONSIDERATIONS

Some basic safety guidelines to follow when weight training in order to gain maximum results without the set back of injuries. Maximize your time when working out by not having any 'down-time' from overuse injuries or excessive soreness (eccentric contraction workouts only).

1. Do not exercise alone
2. Avoid holding your breath especially when lifting overhead
3. Don't hyperventilate. Inhale with the preparation for the lift and exhale with the work. Blow the weight up!
4. If using free weights, keep the hands dry. Check the collars and plates on the weights for security.
5. Be properly warmed up with some easy aerobic activity, stretching and some light lifting before intensity
6. Make sure spotters are available (free weights) and be aware of others around you
7. If using a machine, secure the pin selector
8. When lifting a free weight from the floor or rack, keep the weight close to your body, and use your legs with the correct form

Nutrition for muscle growth lies somewhere between a normal balanced diet of 15% protein of your total caloric intake to the bizarre world of the quick fix and the 'magic' formula. It is important to realize that many of the claims may be unfounded by the scientific research community, since they may not have a vested interest in the outcome of the product. How many studies involved a significant number of participants, hundreds or just a few? Look for the group or sponsors that may be promoting the product, i.e. pills, equipment, supplements, and then make your own determination.

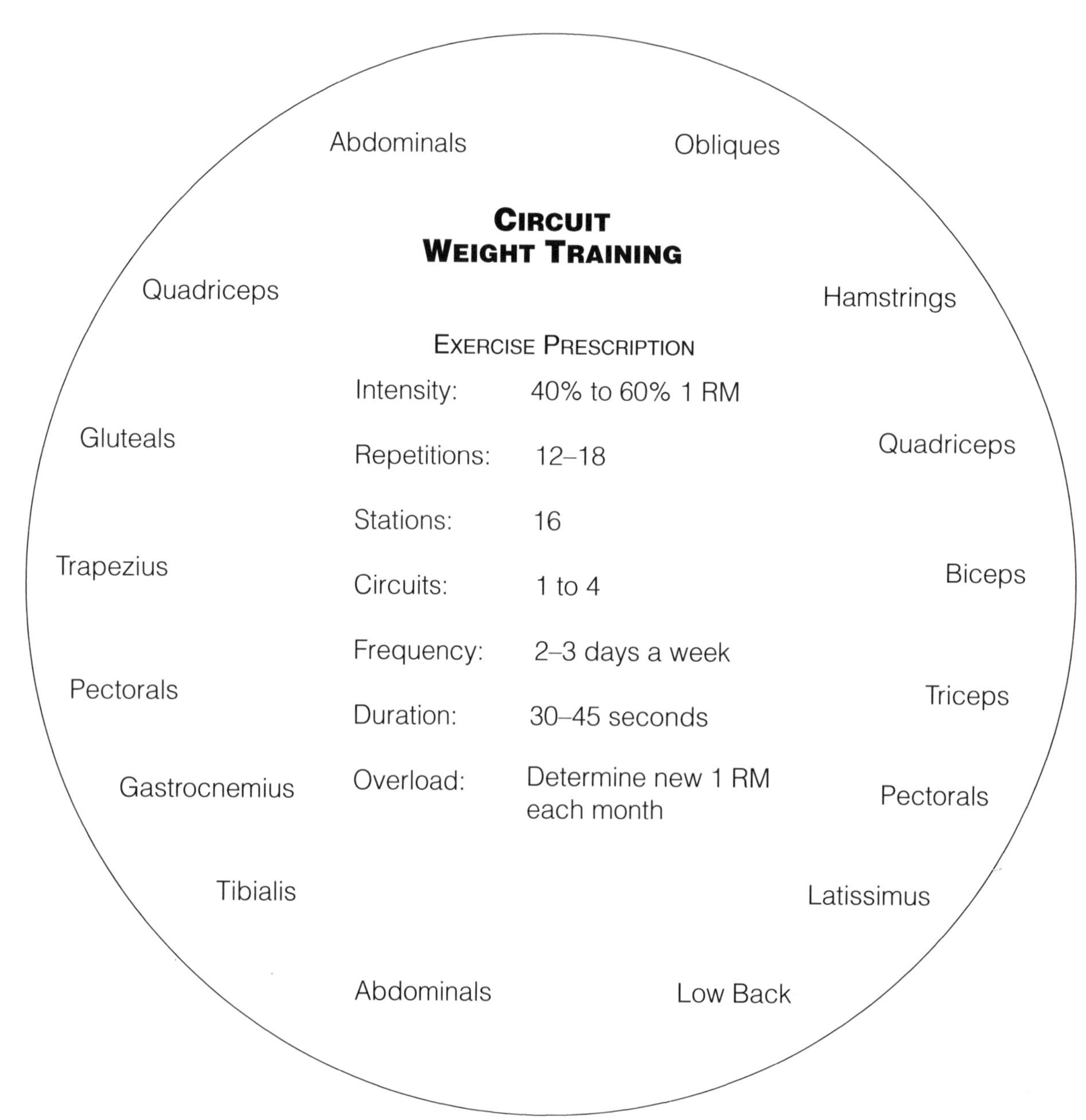

Figure 5.4 CIRCUIT WEIGHT TRAINING

One extreme approach, gaining impetus in the 1980's, in an effort to increase hypertrophy and strength among certain athletes, utilized anabolic steroids (a male sex hormone). There have been numerous attempts by some to gain an edge in competition (football, body building, track and field) through the use of drug enhancing development. Since the idea behind the synthetic hormone injection is to fool the body into developing a higher level of strength as a result of high resistance work than could be accomplished with a normal protein diet. As hypertrophy occurs in the muscle, along with increased strength, some other negative side effects are the result of steroid use.

Some long term health risks are potentially life threatening to not as serious, but you would never know which if you used. Various cancers, liver disorders, hypertension, sex organ changes, secondary sex characteristics, thinning hair, voice change, skin rashes, and aggressive personality demonstrate the variety of problems. Most steroids are not medically supervised and are obtained illegally. The price that a person pays to gain an edge without working up to it, through time and effort, certainly seem steep considering the final score.

The beginner would start at a lower weight with more reps and less sets. As adaptation occurs, you could increase the percentage, decrease the reps and increase the sets. Allow 48 hours for recovery when working near maximum for the same muscle group.

F.I.T. FORMULA FOR MUSCLE STRENGTH
F = 3+ Days Per Week
I = 70%+ of Your 1 RM
T = 2–5 Sets of 4–10 Reps

F.I.T. FORMULA FOR MUSCLE ENDURANCE
F = 3+ Days per Week
I = 40–60% 1 RM
T = 2–4 Sets of 20–40 Reps, with Little Recovery Each Set

F.I.T. FORMULA FOR MUSCLE HYPERTROPHY
F = 3+ Days Per Week
I = 70–85% 1 RM
T = 3–6 Sets of 6–10 Reps

F.I.T. FORMULA FOR MUSCLE TONE
F = 3+ Days Per Week
I = 50–70% 1 RM
T = 2–3 Sets of 15–20 Reps, with Little Recovery Each Set

WORKSHEET 5

NAME ____________________

Muscle Strength

PROBLEM-SOLVING

A person has **low back pain**, possibly due to a muscle imbalance. Describe 2 different exercises that could be done to **strengthen** the **opposing muscle group**? (Not *stretching* exercises.)

1.

2.

(COMPLETE THE OTHER SIDE)

Muscle Endurance

PROBLEM-SOLVING

A runner may need to increase the muscle endurance of the **legs.** In order to maintain muscle balance, indicate 2 *different exercises* for improving one pair of **antagonistic muscles:**

Muscle(s) ____________________

1. ____________________ 2. ____________________

Opposing Muscle(s) ____________________

1. ____________________ 2. ____________________

Muscle Endurance Test

SIXTY-SECOND BENT-KNEE CURL-UPS

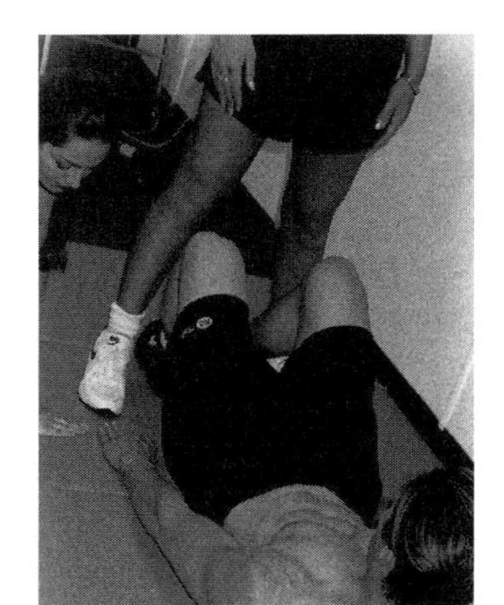

PURPOSE: To measure abdominal muscle endurance.

EQUIPMENT: Stop watch, towel/mat.

PROCEDURE: The students will lie on their back, knees bent, and feet flat. Arms extended by the hips, with hands touching the floor. Curl forward, keeping hands in contact with the floor. (Fingers must move 3″ approximately the width of a hand) Return to starting position with shoulders touching floor.

SCORING: Partner counts the number of correct sit-ups performed in 60-seconds. Incorrect sit-ups include; Failure to move fingers 3″ or failure to return shoulders to the floor.

Fitness Category	Age in Years					
	<20	20–29	30–39	40–49	50–59	>60
Men						
Excellent	>51	>47	>43	>39	>35	>30
Good	48–50	44–46	40–42	35–38	30–34	24–29
Average	39–47	37–43	33–39	28–34	22–29	18–23
Below Average	36–38	33–36	30–32	24–27	19–21	15–17
Poor	<35	<32	<29	<23	<18	<14
Women						
Excellent	>46	>44	>35	>29	>24	>17
Good	36–45	38–43	29–34	24–28	20–23	11–16
Average	30–35	31–37	24–28	20–23	12–19	5–10
Below Average	28–29	27–30	20–23	14–18	10–11	3–4
Poor	<27	<26	<19	<13	<9	<2

Source: Saddleback College

CURL-UPS ______________ FITNESS CATEGORY ______________

LAB 3

Muscle Endurance Test (MEN)

PUSH-UPS

PURPOSE: To measure the endurance of pectorals and triceps.

EQUIPMENT: Towel or mat.

PROCEDURE: *Keeping the body straight*, lower the body until your elbows flex to 90° then return to straight arm position.

SCORING: Partner counts the number of correct non-stop push-ups. Incorrect push-ups: Failure to keep body straight from heels to head throughout the movement; Failure to straighten arms as body is raised.

Fitness Category	Age in Years					
	18–25	26–35	36–45	46–55	56–65	65+
Excellent	>51	>43	>37	>31	>28	>17
Good	35–50	30–42	25–36	21–30	18–27	17–26
Average	19–34	17–29	13–24	11–20	9–17	6–16
Below Average	4–18	4–16	2–12	1–10	0–8	0–5
Poor	<3	<3	<1	<0		

Source: Saddleback College

PUSH-UPS ____________ FITNESS CATEGORY ____________

Muscle Endurance Test (WOMEN)

PUSH-UPS

PURPOSE: To measure the endurance of pectorals and triceps.

EQUIPMENT: Towel or mat.

PROCEDURE: *Keeping the body straight*, lower the body until your elbows flex 90°; return to straight arm position. A modified-position may also be performed from the knees.

SCORING: Partner counts the number of correct non-stop push-ups. Incorrect push-ups: Failure to keep body straight from heels to head throughout the movement; Failure to straighten arms as body is raised.

MODIFIED PUSH-UP NORMS FOR WOMEN

Fitness Category	Age in Years					
	18–25	26–35	36–45	46–55	56–65	65+
Excellent	>34	>33	>32	>28	>23	>21
Good	22–33	23–32	21–31	18–27	15–22	13–20
Average	10–21	12–22	11–20	8–17	7–14	5–12
Below Average	0–9	1–11	0–10	0–7	0–6	0–4
Poor		0				

STANDARD PUSH-UP NORMS FOR WOMEN

Fitness Category	Age in Years					
	18–25	26–35	36–45	46–55	56–65	65+
Excellent	25+	23+	18+	14+	10+	5+
Good	20–24	18–22	14–17	10–13	7–9	3–4
Average	14–19	12–17	9–13	6–9	5–6	1–2
Below Average	9–13	7–11	5–8	3–5	3–4	0
Poor	0–8	0–6	0–4	0–2	0–2	0

Source: Saddleback College

PUSH-UPS ____________ FITNESS CATEGORY ____________

LAB 3

Muscular Strength Test

1 REPETITION MAXIMUM BENCH PRESS

PURPOSE: To measure the muscular strength of the upper body in 1RM.

EQUIPMENT: Bench Press. Calculator.

PROCEDURE: Estimate the weight that an individual can press in one maximum effort. Each student will press the weight once for an easy warm-up. Progressively increase the resistance until the weight stack can no longer be lifted, to a full extension.

SCORING: The score for this test is the maximum number of pounds lifted in one repetition.

Fitness Category	Age in Years					
	<20	20–29	30–39	40–49	50–59	60+
Men						
Excellent	>1.30	>1.20	>1.10	>1.00	>.90	>.75
Good	1.10–1.30	1.05–1.20	.95–1.10	.85–1.00	.75–.90	.60–.75
Average	.73–1.09	.70–1.04	.65–.94	.60–.84	.55–.74	.45–.59
Below Average	.50–.72	.47–.69	.45–.64	.40–.59	.35–.54	.30–.44
Poor	<.50	<.47	<.45	<.40	<.35	<.30
Women						
Excellent	>.80	>.75	>.68	>.63	>.55	>.50
Good	.70–.80	.65–.75	.58–.68	.52–.63	.44–.55	.40–.50
Average	.50–.69	.47–.64	.44–.57	.40–.51	.37–.43	.34–.39
Below Average	.35–.49	.33–.46	.30–.43	.27–.39	.25–.36	.22–.33
Poor	<.35	<.33	<.30	<.27	<.25	<.22

Source: Saddleback College

1 RM BENCH PRESS (amount lifted) ________ ÷ YOUR BODY WEIGHT ________ =

BENCH PRESS WEIGHT RATIO ________ FITNESS CATEGORY ________

LAB 3

Muscular Strength Test

1 REPETITION MAXIMUM LEG PRESS

PURPOSE: To measure the muscular strength of the lower body in 1RM.

EQUIPMENT: Leg Press. Calculator.

PROCEDURE: Estimate the weight that an individual can press in one maximum effort. Each student will press the weight once for any easy warm-up. Progressively increase the resistance until the weight stack can no longer be lifted to a full extension. Adjust the seat/feet position to keep the knees at a 90° angle at the start.

SCORING: The score for this test is the maximum number of pounds lifted in one repetition.

Fitness Category	Age in Years					
	<20	20–29	30–39	40–49	50–59	>60
Men						
Excellent	>2.00	>1.85	>1.70	>1.60	>1.40	>1.30
Good	1.75–2.00	1.65–1.85	1.55–1.70	1.45–1.60	1.25–1.40	1.20–1.30
Average	1.50–1.74	1.40–1.64	1.32–1.54	1.28–1.44	1.15–1.24	1.10–1.19
Below Average	1.25–1.49	1.20–1.39	1.15–1.31	1.10–1.27	1.05–1.14	1.00–1.09
Poor	<1.25	<1.20	<1.15	<1.10	<1.05	<1.00
Women						
Excellent	>1.70	>1.60	>1.50	>1.30	>1.20	>1.10
Good	1.50–1.69	1.40–1.60	1.28–1.50	1.20–1.30	1.12–1.20	1.03–1.10
Average	1.30–1.49	1.22–1.39	1.15–1.27	1.10–1.19	1.04–1.11	.95–1.02
Below Average	1.15–1.29	1.10–1.21	1.05–1.14	1.00–1.09	.95–1.03	.90–.94
Poor	<1.15	<1.10	<1.05	<1.00	<.95	<.90

Source: Saddleback College

1 RM LEG PRESS (amount lifted) __________ ÷ YOUR BODY WEIGHT __________ =

LEG PRESS WEIGHT RATIO __________ FITNESS CATEGORY __________

Glossary of Terms

Agonist is the muscle which directly engages in an action around a joint which has another muscle that can provide an opposing action (antagonist).

Anabolic steroids are a group of synthetic, testosterone-like hormones that promote muscle hypertrophy. Their use in athletics is considered unethical and carries numerous serious health risks.

Antagonist is a muscle that can provide an opposing action to the action of another muscle (the agonist) around a joint.

Atrophy is a reduction in size, or wasting away, of a body part, organ, tissue or cell.

Circuit training is a series of exercises, performed one after the other, with little rest between. Resistance training in this manner increases strength while making some contribution to cardiovascular endurance, as well.

Concentric is a muscle action in which the muscle is shortening under its own power. This action is commonly called "positive" work, or redundantly, "concentric contraction".

Eccentric is the muscle action in which the muscle resists while it is forced to lengthen. This action is commonly called "negative" work, or "eccentric contraction" but, since the muscle is lengthening, the word "contraction" is misapplied.

Extension is a movement which moves the two ends of a jointed body part away from each other, as in straightening the arm.

Fast twitch fibers are a type of muscle fiber that contracts quickly and is used in most intensive, short duration exercises, such as weightlifting or sprints.

Flexion is a movement which moves the two ends of a jointed body part closer to each other, as in bending the arm.

Hypertrophy is an enlargement of a body part or organ by the increase in size of the cells that make it up.

Isokinetic is a muscle contraction against a resistance that moves a constant velocity, so that the maximum force of which the muscle is capable throughout the range of motion may be applied.

Isometric is muscle action in which the muscle attempts to contract against a fixed limit. (No muscle movement)

Isotonic is a muscle contraction against a constant resistance, as in lifting a weight.

Motor neuron is a nerve cell which conducts impulses from the central nervous system to a group of muscle fibers to-produce movement

Muscle group are specific muscles that act together at the same joint to produce a movement.

One repetition max (1 RM) is the maximum resistance with which a person can execute one repetition of an exercise movement.

Overload is subjecting a part of the body to efforts greater than it is accustomed to, in order to elicit a training response. Increases may be in intensity or duration.

Periodization is a training technique used mostly by highly trained competitive athletes. The purpose is to reach a maximum or peak performance at a specific time.

Progressive resistance is exercise in which the amount of resistance is increased to further stress the muscle after it has become accustomed to handling a lesser resistance.

Repetition is an individual completed exercise movement. Repetitions are usually done in multiples. Resistance is the force which a muscle is required to work against.

Resistance is the force which a muscle is required to work against.

Set is a group of repetitions of an exercise movement done consecutively, without rest, until a given number, or momentary exhaustion is reached.

Slow twitch is a type of muscle fiber that contracts slowly and is used most in moderate intensity, endurance exercises, such as distance running.

Strength is the amount of muscular force that can be exerted.

Testosterone is a sex hormone that predominates in the male, is responsible for the development of male secondary sex characteristics and is involved in the hypertrophy of muscle.

Related Websites

National Strength & Conditioning Assn.
www.nsca-lift.org

American College of Sports-Medicine
www.acsm.org

Muscle Strength and Endurance
www.exrx.net
www.inestrong.com
www.healthlive.com

Fitness FAQ's
www.getbig.com
www.afpafitness.com
www.lifeclinic.com

Study Questions

Name ______________________________

1. If you are trying to develop a weight training program to improve your strength or endurance, what would you use as an indicator of your beginning strength?

2. Give examples of the Principles of Training for application to improving muscle strength. Any differences for muscle endurance?

3. How would the ratio of muscle fibers differ in the following athletes? a) sprinter b) marathon runner c) wrestler d) power lifter. Is this ratio primarily a result of heredity, training, or both? Why?

Skill-Related Fitness

KEY TERMS

Agility	Freestyle-Back
Balance	Freestyle-Front
Breast Stroke	Power
Coordination	Reaction Time
Elementary Backstroke	Side Stroke
Float	Speed

SKILL-RELATED FITNESS

Skill-related fitness is also referred to as motor ability or sports fitness. Motor ability skills include: Agility, Balance, Coordination, Power, Speed, and Reaction Time. Some people are better in one area than another. Good combinations and proficiency in these areas makes someone more skilled in various sports. You can avoid injuries and improve your performance with good skill-related fitness. In everyday life, people are more accident-prone when they don't possess good skill-related fitness ability. Anyone can improve their motor abilities!

Locomotor skills include: Walking, Running, Hopping, Leaping, Sliding, Jumping, Skipping, and Galloping. All of these skills and motor ability have other aspects related to performance such as distance and depth perception; kinesthetic sense, and visual tracking. Sub-components would be eye-hand coordination (tennis), and eye-foot coordination (soccer).

All behavior is based on motor skills. These motor skills are developed as early as prenatal stages. These basic skills form the foundation for performance and locomotor skills for daily tasks. Many children

LOCOMOTOR MOVEMENTS

Walk

A natural walk is a movement which carries the body through space by a transference of weight from one foot to another.

Run

The run pattern is much like that of a walk; however there is a period of no support in the run.

Source: Saddleback College

Figure 6.1 Leap

Leap

The leap is much the same as the run; however in a leap the ankle and knee actions are increased so that a more upward motion is achieved.

Jump

A jump is a motion which carries the body through the air from a take-off from one or both feet.

Hop

The body is pushed off the floor from one foot and after a slight suspension in the air it is returned to the floor with the weight taken on the same foot.

Slide

A slide is a combination of a step and a leap.

Gallop

A gallop is when the same foot leads and the sliding pattern is done in a forward or backward direction.

Skip

The skip is a combination of the walk and the hop.

have a low level of locomotor skills in the early elementary grades. Repeated practice is essential in acquiring proficiency, and greater retention of skills is promoted by overlearning. Learn through experience. A good beginning is through playing games.

Efficiency of movement is the ultimate goal in all play and work. Studies have shown that an individual who is highly skilled in motor activities is also more popular, of higher intelligence, and better adjusted. Although most of the basic movement patterns are established by five years old, individuals can still refine skills into a mature pattern of motor ability.

BALANCE AS A PART OF FITNESS

According to Running and Fit News, March 1995, most of us don't think about balance unless we develop a problem with it, such as vertigo, which can be caused by inner ear problems, some drugs, or certain infectious diseases. In recent years interest in balance has grown to the point that we might now describe complete fitness as including endurance, strength, flexibility, and balance. Just like the more familiar fitness components, balance tends to decrease with age, and is impaired by injury and must be retrained.

First, let's get a feel for the role of balance in our activities. Walking is simple enough but involves having only one foot at a time in contact with the ground. Consequently, there is a balance component in walking, even though we don't think about it.

Running involves periods with both feet off the ground punctuated by single foot-strikes. In running, too, we don't think about balance much, except maybe when racing a steep downhill with a sharp curve; then balance is an important part of the skills needed for good performance in many sports.

By analogy with endurance, strength, and flexibility, it is logical to expect that if you practice balance exercises you will improve your balance, and perhaps your performance in some sports.

The simplest lower body balance exercise is standing on one leg. Not everyone agrees this is of practical value, arguing that standing on one leg only teaches you to stand on one leg. However, many physical therapists teach it as a starting point.

You can stand on one leg with the other held in front, to the side, or behind your body for variations. As soon as you get the hang of this, stand on one leg with your eyes closed for as long as you can. You will find this more difficult. The reason is that part of your balance response occurs through a signal loop from your eyes which feed information to your balance system and tell it how you are moving with respect to your surroundings. If you deactivate the loop by closing your eyes, you are performing a pure balance exercise without external aid from your surroundings.

After a while you should become quite proficient. You can continue to develop your balance by switching from hard to softer surfaces, ending up on a foam cushion or trampoline.

Visit a rehabilitation facility and you may see balance devices, used to help rehabilitate injured ankles or knees, which impair normal balance.

A balance or rocker board is a board or platform mounted on a ball or inflatable ring (resembling an inner tube). You can begin by standing on both legs and with low air pressure. By increasing the air pressure you make the board harder to control. After a while you can try standing on one leg. When you can control the board on one leg you can give the pressure a boost to make the exercise more demanding. Perform these gyrations with your eyes closed for maximal benefit.

© ayakovlevcom/Shutterstock.com

COMPONENTS OF SKILL-RELATED FITNESS

Training for all of the skill-related areas involves the very basic principles of specificity. To improve in any one of the components, you must train for improvement in that very movement. Sometimes it may relate to repetitions of the factor, however, it is not just the practice, but to perfect the practice as a goal.

Agility

The ability to change direction quickly with controlled movement, with precision and no wasted movement, or loss of balance. Pure strength and aerobic conditioning are not a factor, however performance may diminish as fatigue occurs particularly with balance. Excess weight may also be a hindrance.

Balance

The ability to maintain control of equilibrium in a variety of static positions and dynamic movements. Training in a specific activity will bring about improved performance—gymnastics, golf, diving, tennis, basketball, rock climbing.

Coordination

The ability of the senses and the body to function harmoniously to produce complex movements. Practice the correct skill or activity to improve.

Power

The ability to use strength to apply force quickly. All sports performances utilize some form of power. Ability to improve movement time—strength with speed of application.

Reaction Time

The ability to initiate action rapidly following a stimulus to move, (starting gun, whistle, voice command). Training incorporates repeated responses with more awareness of concentration stimulus only, and eliminate any extraneous distractions.

Speed

The ability to perform a movement or cover a distance in a short period of time. (Movement time). Total or overall speed would combine your reaction time to the stimulus and how well you move. Training could include strength, lower fat to lean ratio.

SKILL-RELATED ACTIVITIES

LEVEL OF MOTOR-ABILITY IN SPORTS

Recreational Sports	Agility	Balance	Coordination	Power	Speed	Reaction Time
Basketball	High	Low	High	Med.	Med.	Med.
Golf	Low	Med.	High	Low	Low	Low
Martial Arts	Med.	High	High	Med.	Med.	Med.
Racquetball	High	Med.	High	Low	Med.	High
Rollerblading	Low	High	Med.	Low	Low	Low
Softball	Med.	Low	High	Med.	High	Med.
Tennis	High	Med.	High	Med.	High	High
Water Skiing	Low	High	Med.	Low	Low	Low

An optimum level of skill-related fitness is important to survival, and the dangerous situations one may encounter.

1. Reaction time and speed for running to escape an oncoming car, or being pursued.
2. Swimming after falling into the water, or struggling to survive in a flood.
3. Entrapment in a burning house.
4. Injury or containment in a car, train, or airplane and delayed rescue.
5. Unusual or prolonged physical activity—resulting from a natural catastrophe.

LAB 4

Agility Test

AGILITY RUN

PURPOSE: To measure the ability to change direction to gross body movements accurately and quickly while moving fast.

EQUIPMENT: 3 boxes or cones in a row, 9′ in between, & stopwatch.

PROCEDURE: Stand in forward stride position, front foot just behind line. On signal "Go" run the course as fast as possible, touching foot beyond end lines.

SCORING: Time to complete the course is determined by stopwatch. Score is the number of seconds, to the nearest tenth, from the starting "Go" until the finish line is crossed.

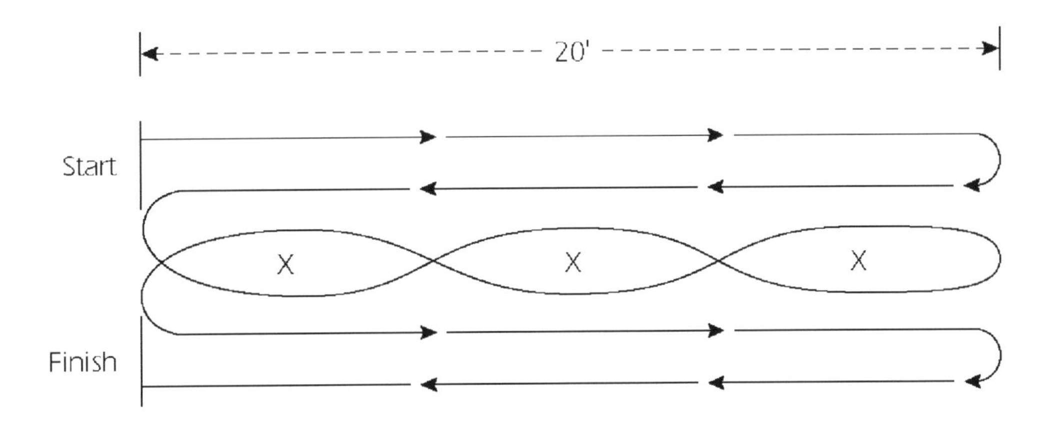

AGILITY TEST

MEN

FITNESS CATEGORY	<29	30–39	40–49	50–59	60+
Excellent	<12.6	<13.6	<14.6	<15.6	<16.6
Good	12.7–13.3	13.7–14.3	14.7–15.3	15.7–16.3	16.7–17.3
Average	13.4–14.8	14.4–15.8	15.4–16.8	16.4–17.8	17.4–18.8
Below Average	14.9–15.2	15.9–16.2	16.9–17.2	17.9–18.2	18.9–19.2
Poor	>15.2	>16.2	>17.2	>18.2	>19.2

WOMEN

FITNESS CATEGORY	<29	30–39	40–49	50–59	60+
Excellent	<14.0	<15.0	<16.0	<17.0	<18.0
Good	14.4–14.8	15.1–15.8	16.1–16.8	17.1–17.8	18.1–18.8
Average	14.9–17.8	15.9–18.8	16.9–19.8	17.9–20.8	18.9–21.8
Below Average	17.9–18.7	18.9–19.7	19.9–20.7	20.9–21.7	21.9–22.7
Poor	>18.7	>19.7	>20.7	>21.7	>22.7

Source: Saddleback College

SCORE ______________ FITNESS CATEGORY ______________

FIGURE-8 AGILITY RUN

PURPOSE: To measure the ability to change direction of gross body movements accurately and quickly while moving rapidly.

EQUIPMENT: A gym floor is recommended. A stop watch and five obstacles, (chairs, cones). Cones set 6′ × 10′. 4 Cones set 6′ × 10′ apart and 1 Cone in Center.

PROCEDURE: From a standing start, run once around the obstacles placed as shown below. Starting signal is "on your mark", "get set," "go."

SCORING: Time to complete the course is determined with a stopwatch. Score is the number of seconds to the nearest tenth, from the starting "go" until the finish line is crossed. One practice is okay.

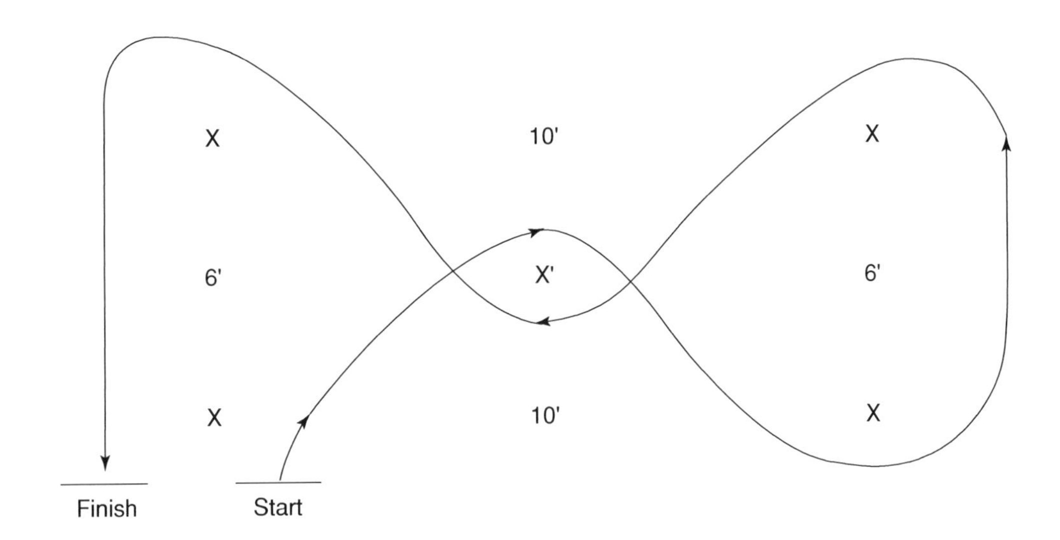

FIGURE-8 AGILITY RUN

MEN

FITNESS CATEGORY	<29	30–39	40–49	50–59	60+
Excellent	<4.7	<5.7	<6.7	<7.7	<8.7
Good	4.8–4.9	5.8–5.9	6.8–6.9	7.8–7.9	8.8–8.9
Average	5.0–5.2	6.0–6.2	7.0–7.2	8.0–8.2	9.0–9.2
Below Average	5.3–5.5	6.3–6.5	7.3–7.5	8.3–8.5	9.3–9.5
Poor	>5.6	>6.6	>7.6	>8.6	>9.6

WOMEN

FITNESS CATEGORY	<29	30–39	40–49	50–59	60+
Excellent	<5.3	<6.3	<7.3	<8.3	<9.3
Good	5.4–5.6	6.4–6.6	7.4–7.6	8.4–8.6	9.4–9.6
Average	5.7–5.9	6.7–6.9	7.7–7.9	8.7–8.9	9.7–9.9
Below Average	6.0–6.2	7.0–7.2	8.0–8.2	9.0–9.2	10.0–10.2
Poor	>6.3	>7.3	>8.3	>8.3	>10.3

Source: Saddleback College

SCORE ______________ FITNESS CATEGORY ______________

LAB 4

Balance Test (Dynamic)

PURPOSE: To measure dynamic balance, the ability to maintain equilibrium in an upright and moving direction.

EQUIPMENT: Two 8′ × 4″ Wood Balance Beams, joined at one end at a 45 degree angle.

PROCEDURE: Place shoe lengthwise on the long axis of the beam, with hands placed on hips. Walk forward maintaining balance until you reach the end of second beam. Pivot, and return, walking forward to the start. Now walk backwards until you reach the end of the second beam.

SCORING: Errors = each time the hands leave the hips or stepping on the floor.

RESULTS: ERRORS ______________ RATING ______________

BALANCE BEAM RATINGS

Excellent	0 Errors	=	5 Points
Good	1 Error	=	4 Points
Average	2 Errors	=	3 Points
Below Average	3 Errors	=	2 Points
Poor	4 Errors	=	1 Points

LAB 4

Balance Test (Static)

Photo taken by Jan Duquette

PURPOSE: To measure static balance (maintaining equilibrium in a stationary position).

EQUIPMENT: Stop Watch.

PROCEDURE: With eyes closed, hands on the hips, lift the opposite foot from the floor, maintaining balance. When balance is felt, person being tested signals start by saying "Go", at which time stop watch is started. Time is stopped when person touches floor with any part of the body or when either hand is removed from the hip. Foot must remain in contact with the floor at all times.

SCORING: Score is the total number of seconds in which balance is held. Time stops when hands leave hips or foot touches floor, or eyes open.

RESULTS: Right ________ + Left ________ = ________ Seconds RATING ________

BALANCE TEST RATINGS

FITNESS CATEGORY		MEN	WOMEN
Excellent	(5 Points)	11.7-7.7	12.0-7.5
Good	(4 Points)	7.6-5.6	7.4-5.5
Average	(3 Points)	5.5-5.0	5.4-4.4
Below Average	(2 Points)	4.9-4.0	4.3-3.5
Poor	(1 Point)	3.9 or Less	3.5 or Less Points

LAB 4

Power Test

STANDING LONG JUMP

PURPOSE: To measure the power of the legs.

EQUIPMENT: Mat with markings down the center, or tape measure.

PROCEDURE: Stand with feet several inches apart, centered with the line, toes just behind the takeoff line. Prior to jump, swing your arms backward and bend your knees. Perform the jump by extending your knees and swinging your arms forward at the same time.

SCORING: Distance is recorded from the takeoff line to the heel or other body part that touches the floor nearest the takeoff line. Three trials are allowed, and the best trial measure to the nearest inch becomes the final score.

Long Jump

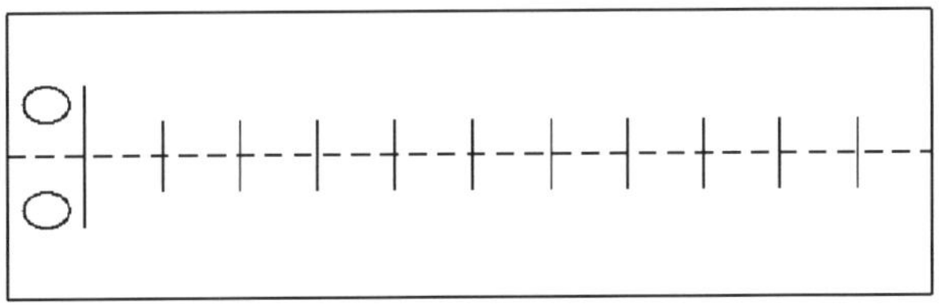

POWER TEST

MEN

FITNESS CATEGORY	<29	30–39	40–49	50–59	60+
Excellent	>7′8	>7′2	>6′2	>5′2	>4′2
Good	7′1–7′6	6′7–7′1	5′7–6′1	4′7–5′1	3′7–4′1
Average	6′6–7′0	6′2–6′6	5′2–5′6	4′2–4′6	3′2–3′6
Below Average	6′2–6′5	5′8–6′1	4′8–5′1	3′8–4′1	2′8–3′1
Poor	<6′1	<5′7	<4′7	<3′7	<2′7

WOMEN

FITNESS CATEGORY	<29	30–39	40–49	50–59	60+
Excellent	>6′0	>5′0	>4′0	>3′0	>2′0
Good	5′10–5′11	4′10–4′11	3′10–3′11	2′10–2′11	1′10–1′11
Average	5′5–5′9	4′5–4′9	3′5–3′9	2′5–2′9	1′5–1′9
Below Average	5′0–5′4	4′0–4′4	3′0–3′4	2′–2′4	1′–1′4
Poor	>4′11	>3′11	>2′11	>1′11	>11″

Source: Saddleback College

SCORE ______________ FITNESS CATEGORY ______________

SWIMMING: SAFETY AND FUNDAMENTALS

Swimming is undoubtedly one of man's earliest athletic activities. Pictures of swimmers were carved on the rock walls of caves in the Libyan Desert in the era of about 9000 B.C. Some historians believe man learned to swim in order to survive. It is surmised that man was forced into the water by wild animals. Then, in order to stay afloat, he extended his arms, paddled the water, and kept his legs moving in a running fashion.

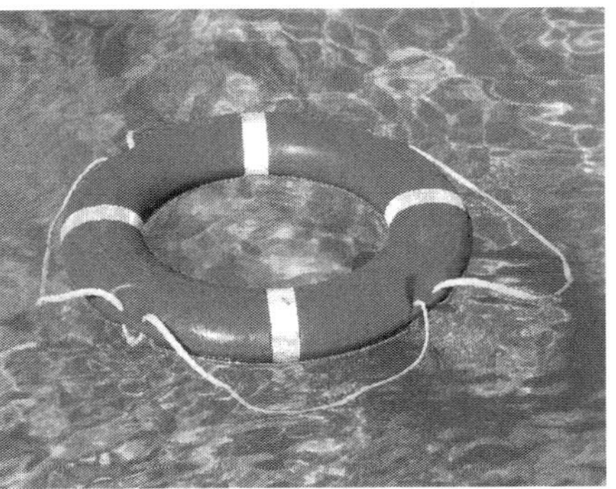

© untitled/Shutterstock.com

Water Safety

Personal Safety in Swimming

1. Make a serious effort to learn to swim before engaging in activities involving the water.
2. Swim only in supervised areas, in the presence of others—NEVER SWIM ALONE!
3. Remain in waters well within your own capabilities.
4. Fatigue comes about more readily in the first swim of the season; therefore, distance swims should be avoided at that time.
5. When entering cold water, a swimmer should adjust gradually by splashing water over the body.
6. The length of time the bather stays in the water is governed by a sense of physical comfort.
7. Should cramps occur and the swimmer is unable to get out of the water, he should roll to a face-down position in the water, lungs fully inflated, grasp the cramped area, and apply pressure firmly with one or both hands.
8. A swimmer caught in any type of current should never try to "go for it". Swim diagonally across the current with its flow (the longest way home may mean the safest way home).
9. The swimmer should avoid forcibly blowing water from the nose.
10. Individuals with skin disease, inflamed eyes, nasal or ear discharge, cuts, scratches, or any communicable disease should refrain from swimming.
11. "Horseplay" in, or about the water is unwise.
12. A swimmer should always "stop, look, and listen," before entering the water.
13. Don't overestimate your ability as a swimmer and take foolish chances in the water. Learn to respect the water.

Safe Bathing Places Should Have:

1. A good bottom that is smooth and slopes gently toward deep water.
2. An approach to the water that is free from rocks, stumps, sudden "step-offs," and sunken logs.
3. An absence of currents, whirlpools, and the like.
4. Some form of lifesaving equipment located nearby.

© Epic Stock/Shutterstock.com

Front Freestyle

The front freestyle or crawl stroke is the fastest and most efficient stroke in swimming. More people use this stroke than any other. The position that you place your body in the water should lend itself to becoming very hydro-dynamic. Maximize the strength and flexibility of the arms, shoulders, & legs by using the flutter kick. This kick consists of a downbeat with a movement originating at the hip in a forceful downward motion of the thigh with the lower leg and ankle relaxed and toes pointed in. As the opposite leg is involved in the upbeat, the thigh from the hip down is active in an upward sweeping motion, still keeping the lower leg relaxed & passing by the other leg you then initiate the downbeat.

A common mistake is the bending of the knees/heels out of water. Trying to keep the head out of the water will drop the lower body deeper in the water becoming less efficient and not as streamlined. Another misconception is that if you kick harder you will increase your forward speed and yet, for a longer distance you will expend more energy with harder kicking, with fatigue not far behind.

Correct positioning of the body is to become horizontal with the water surface and maintain the waterline at the top of the forehead keeping the face in the water. The arm action is two parts. Above the water the arm is relaxed with the elbow flexed and high in a sweeping motion coming up from the thigh until the hand reaches for the water forward from the shoulder. There should be a slight rolling motion of the body in the direction of the elbow coming out of water. This movement will facilitate the pattern of breathing you select. As the hand enters the water with the palm facing outward slightly and the fingers closed, you press your arm down and slightly outward. The strongest part of the pull occurs after being straight down as the flexed arm moves from the chest to the waist and prepares to begin again. Don't hold your breath, but exhale very slowly and then inhale on your desired side just as the arm recovers with the elbow high. Keeping your face in the water and by rolling your body from side to side allows the head and water movement to form a small pocket of air at the mouth.

© Schmid Christopher/Shutterstock.com

Back Freestyle

The back freestyle or back crawl stroke is very similar to the front free except you are on your back. Body position is nearly the same to maintain—almost horizontal with the back of the head in the water. The hips are not elevated as high as in the front free since during the flutter kick, the upbeat action of the legs would cause the thighs to break the surface of the water reducing efficiency. Alternating the leg action is the same: the upper leg lifting up and a lower leg relaxed with toes pointed in, almost touching the toes of the opposite leg as they pass by. Try not to lift the knees too forcefully coming out of the water but let the lower leg and foot create the pressure on the water as they come near the surface. In this last phase of the up beat, the foot is kicking slightly out because of the rolling action of the body as the arm is reaching up and back.

Extend the arm overhead in a relaxed manner entering the water above the shoulder as the body rolls to that side. With the hand turned out and the edge of the hand entering the water, the arm moves in a sweeping motion until approaching the side of the body. The hand will continue to rotate until it reaches a backward facing position near the surface of the water. The elbow will flex to a near right angle as the hand completes its sweep. Breathing in the back freestyle is usually not a problem since you have the top of your head in the water. For maximum efficiency and minimum use of extra unwanted energy output, breathing is to be kept rhythmical and usually with each arm stroke.

© Sergey Peterman/Shutterstock.com

Breast Stroke

The following strokes are going to be considered as an efficient means of movement and not from a speed or fast mode of swimming. First will be the breast stroke. Again, your body position should be as streamlined as much as possible during the stroke. At the conclusion of the kick, the body should be in alignment with the legs extended together as well as the arms stretched out in front together (glide position). Breathing occurs once during a complete arm and leg stroke cycle. Inhaling at the conclusion of the arm stroke action and then exhaling slowly during the remainder of the cycle.

The type of kick used in the breast stroke is different from the flutter and can be called a "whip" or a "frog" kick as a vague description of the movement. From an extended position (glide) the legs recover by flexing the knee and then the hip. As the heels approach the buttocks in a shoulder wide stance, the legs are extended outward in a sweeping manner that is completed when the kick goes out, back and then finally together. It is important to keep the ankles flexed at the beginning of the recovery and then slowly rotate them outwardly during the sweep and finish up facing inward and fully extended.

The arm stroke is employed at the conclusion of the whip kick. From an extended position, the arms are brought back in a sweeping motion with the palms facing out. As the arms pass the shoulders, the hands are pressed forcefully back as they continue the arc until they come up and under the chin. At the finish of this movement, the hands will rotate inward under the chin and then extended straight out in a "glide" position but now facing slightly out. The timing between the arms and the legs do not overlap. When you bring the arms up under the chin after the power move and you take your breath, the legs will be recovering and getting ready to "whip" kick you into a fully extended position. A common error that often occurs is in the "glide". Many swimmers try to go too fast and are constantly pulling the arms forcefully throughout the stroke and ending up with their arms at their sides. When they try to move the hands forward for the arm stroke, they impede their progress by pushing against the water.

Side Stroke

A second type of resting stroke is called the side stroke. As with all the others, the key to efficiency is to maintain a streamlined body alignment in the water at the conclusion of the propulsion action. Since the body is in a relatively horizontal layout with the head on its side in the water—the mouth is above the water line, so breathing is able to be completed easily. If the head is raised above the surface then the hips and legs would sink making the stroke cycle difficult to accomplish.

A different kind of kick is used in the side stroke and is called a "scissors" kick. The extended position of the legs in the "glide" will have the toes pointed backward, the "top" arm beside the body and the "bottom" arm extended out to the front. In the preliminary movement the legs are flexed and brought forward together without undue effort. The top knee is flexed as the heel approaches the buttocks and then the top leg is extended out and to the rear with the sole of the foot applying pressure to the water. The bottom leg flexes so the angle of the knee is extreme and with the toes pointed, this forces water rearward with a squeezing action until the legs are fully extended. This squeezing action or "scissors" movement will provide propulsion.

At the conclusion of the glide, the arm stroke will alternate the force of the top and bottom arms. When the forward momentum begins to fade, the bottom arm sweeps back in a small circular motion until it reaches forward to full extension, all having stayed below the surface of the water.

Which side you face doesn't make a difference. Some people will utilize a top leg rearward and the bottom leg forward in an "inverted scissors" kick. There is no right or wrong method with the kick or

even the arm stroke. A technique called an "overarm side stroke" in which the top arm is reaching over the water until it meets the bottom arm at the chest as in a normal move. It can be more efficient and faster in propulsion since the top arm won't create any drag as it does when moving under the water. This movement is good if you need the added speed or simply a change in the action to reduce any fatigue.

Elementary Back Stroke

The third and final stroke considered is one of the easier to learn and master and known as the "elementary" back stroke. The horizontal layout position on the back is ideal and allows breathing to occur on demand and the kick to be used is identical to the breast stroke except on your back. The body is extended with the arms beside the legs with the toes pointed (glide). The legs are easily brought back and down about shoulder width apart with the knees flexing until the toes are past the knees. Then a sweeping action of the legs initially with the feet facing out and a powerful squeezing of the inner legs to provide the power in the whip kick. As the legs come back together the feet will move from facing out to inward at the finish.

The arm stroke commonly used places the hands under the water surface throughout. From an extended position the hands move up the side of the body by flexing the elbows until reaching the armpits. Then extend the arms outward and pressing the water back in an arc until reaching the body. During this phase, the hands have rotated from palms out on the reach, to palms facing in at the end of the stroke.

Once the propulsion from the arm stroke and the leg kick have occurred, remain in an extended glide and only resume the next cycle when your momentum slows down. Two alternative styles may also be utilized: 1. in the arm stroke you can be reaching overhead with a straight arm, or 2. the whip kick may be completed before the arm stroke provides its force and propulsion (either bent arm or straight arm).

The Float

The ability to float certainly reduces the chances of you becoming a casualty during any type of water exposure. If a victim of a boating accident or involved in a riptide is to survive in deep water for any period of time, knowing how to float will certainly increase your chances.

A good approach to a proper float technique is to roll over on your back and concentrate on being as relaxed as possible, with sufficient amount of air in the lungs. Once in the water, gulp or force as much air into the lungs, and not just in your mouth. Lay back into the water by arching your back and lifting your hips up near the surface. Let your legs widen to about shoulder width with relaxed knees dropping the feet down below the knees. If the arms are at your sides, gradually move them underwater out to shoulder level and let them relax slightly outstretched. It's possible that your ears and even forehead will be under water in this arched yet relaxed position, but the mouth will be above water which will allow you to continue filling the lungs with air, when needed.

The ability to float can be used with any of the aforementioned strokes, intermittently, as a means of recovering from the swimming effort.

LAB 5

Aquatic Ability

SWIMMING TEST

PURPOSE: To measure the ability to swim in deep water.

EQUIPMENT: Pool, deeper than 5 feet.

PROCEDURE: Jump into deep water. Perform the correct stroke for 25 yards as instructed. (One width of the pool). Float will be done *without movement* for a short time.

SWIM TEST						
Strokes Rating	Front Freestyle	Back Freestyle	Breast Stroke	Side Stroke	Elem Back	Float 30 Sec+
Excellent 5 Points						
Good 4 Points						
Average 3 Points						
Below Average 2 Points						
Poor 1 Point						
K = Kick C = Coordination B = Breathing G = Glide						

Worksheet 6

Name ______________________________

Skill-Related Fitness

Since all behavior is based on motor ability, please list five different activities or daily tasks that **you** currently perform, and identify the correct skill-related components involved in each.

Current Activity	Skill-Related Component
1.	
2.	
3.	
4.	
5.	

(COMPLETE THE OTHER SIDE)

AQUATIC SAFETY

Describe 3 different situations in which a person's aquatic knowledge/ability would be beneficial. (Do not include swimming)

1.

2.

3.

List 3 suggestions you would make for someone with children in regards to water safety:

1.

2.

3.

Glossary of Terms

Motor Ability

Agility is the ability to quickly and efficiently change body position and direction.

Balance is the ability to maintain the body in proper equilibrium.

Coordination is the integration of the nervous and the muscular systems to produce correct, graceful, and harmonious body movements.

Power is the ability to produce maximum force in the shortest time.

Reaction time is the time required to initiate a response to a given stimulus.

Speed is the ability to rapidly propel the body or a part of the body from one point to another.

Aquatic Swim Strokes

Breast stroke a swim stroke using arms in a circling motion on your front in the water, with the legs doing a "whip" or "frog" kick.

Elementary back stroke is executed on your back using the arms and legs in unison. Arms extend up to armpits and out, pulling water down to sides, while legs bend from the knees, circling outward and closing.

Float is a life-saving skill done on your back, lying very still and holding your breath.

Freestyle front is the fastest, most efficient stroke in swimming. This is done facing down in the water and alternating your arms in a forward circling manner. Legs are alternating up and down, doing a "flutter kick".

Freestyle back is performed on your back, doing a "flutter kick", while the arms are alternating in a circular motion, pulling down to your sides.

Side stroke is a second type of resting stroke. The body is on the side, and bottom arm extends forward then pulling down, while top arm bends half-way forward, touching other arm and extend down to legs. The legs are doing a "scissor kick".

Related Websites

American Alliance for Health, Physical
Education, Recreation & Dance
www.aahperd.org

Homegrown Fitness
www.fitnessfunctions.com

American Council on Exercise (A.C.E.)
www.acefitness.com

Swimnews
www.swimnews.com

USA Swimmers
www.usaswimming.org

Presiduct's Council on Physical Fitness & Sports
www.fitness.gov

Study Questions

Name ___________________________________

1. What skill-related components would be desired to perform efficiently at Soccer? Snowboarding? Basketball?

2. What are the energy efficient swim strokes that would be useful in saving your life? What type of kick would be used?

Stress Management

KEY TERMS	
Active/Passive training	Psychosomatic
Autogenic training	Stress
Biofeedback	Stressor
Distress	Stress management
Eustress	Time management
Fight or flight	Type A personality
Meditation	Type B personality
Progressive relaxation	Type C personality

Stress is generally defined as a non-specific response of the body to any demand made on it. Coronary heart disease, which is the number one killer in the United States can be caused or aggravated by stress. However, people in good physical condition can withstand more stress. The American Medical Association claims that half of the nations annual $425 billion tab for medical services are due to unhealthy lifestyles.

YOU are most important in determining what you feel. Perceive, analyze, and decide what is important. Stress can be a positive challenge towards your purpose and accomplishments. The basis is balance and control of your environment and your expectations. Controlling unnecessary stress may be the most important key to preventing heart attacks. Make a commitment towards achieving what is best for you. Remember the three C's: Challenge—Control—Commitment.

Stress may be the single greatest contributor to illness. Stress diseases can, and do, kill! If we have high blood pressure it doubles our chances of a heart attack. If we smoke, and have high cholesterol, our

© Login/Shutterstock.com

risk is eight times greater. If we have all three, our chances are twelve times higher! The effects of stress can take its toll on our cardiovascular system, digestive system, our immune system and our skeleto-muscular system.

The cardiovascular system can be affected from stress when we develop arrhythmia—an alteration in rhythm of the heartbeat either in time or force. This condition may lead to hypertension—abnormally high blood pressure, and heart attack risk is increased. More women than men are affected by hypertension, but men sometimes have more migraine headaches.

The digestive system disorders from stress include; ulcers, colitis, constipation, and diarrhea.

The immune system is weakened when we are facing chronic stress. We may feel run-down, develop infections, allergies, viruses, inflammation in our joints, and develop some type of cancers.

The skeletomuscular system is also affected by stress. Muscles and bones are not only used to express feelings, but to repress them. When we overdo stressing our muscles, we may develop chronic muscle spasms. Arthritis is also common with high levels of stress.

Hans Selye, a pioneer in stress research, used the term, General Adaptation Syndrome, as a process which occurs when our body reacts to almost any stressor. The syndrome occurs in three stages—alarm, resistance, and exhaustion.

Alarm, or the fight-or-flight response, is our physiological response when we confront a threat, try to escape from it, or try to recover from it. Our sympathetic nervous system stimulates a discharge of stress hormones epinephrine (adrenaline), and norepinephrine (noradrenaline), from the adrenal glands. Catecholamines are adrenaline-like chemicals which are also released, and a surge of these sometimes kills heart cells. These stress hormones that send emergency signals to the body, also may cause brittle bones in women, infections and even cancer, researchers say. Some forms of depression bring on a similar hormonal state. Dr. Philip Gold of the National Institute of Mental Health, has stated, "If you are in danger, cortisol is good for you . . . But if it becomes unregulated, it can produce disease."

Resistance is a stage following alarm which we encounter if the stressor persists for more than a brief time. Usually our body's systems return to a state of balance or homeostasis. However, if the stressor is intense or chronic, the body enters the final stage, exhaustion. During the exhaustion phase our bodies are more vulnerable to dysfunction and disease, because our immune systems are weakened. Without help or appropriate stress management techniques we can be physically and psychologically damaging our bodies.

It is not the event—but how we view it, which affects our emotional and physiological responses. Our emotional intimacy is strongly depressed with chronic stress. We may develop apathy, anxiety, denial, mental fatigue, and become very irritable. These emotional problems arouse the hypothalamus in the brain (releasing neurochemicals epinephrine and norepinephrine), and the pituitary gland, which stimulates a hormone ACTH, that releases cortisol—and sets off reactions and speeds up the body's metabolism. When our metabolic rate rises, we become nervous, sweaty, and shaky. If our metabolic rate lowers, we become easily tired, cold, and are prone to be overweight.

Modern stress is caused by our modern lifestyles, and technology. One thing we can do is to try and change our mental attitudes. Money is only one mark of success. Some people push so hard to achieve financial success, but in the process lose their balance of harmony between mind and body. Rich people aren't always happy. Time management is popular because people have a difficult time handling all the demands they face throughout the day. Evaluate the potential stressor and appraise it—will it cause more stress, or can it be dealt with? Clarifying your values may be necessary.

Vigilance is a chronic response to a loss of control. Our behavior due to stress may be in extremes—anger, avoidance, administrative, or legal problems. We seem to express our joy freely, and swallow our anger. Talking is therapeutic at all ages, but it is speaking with passion, rather than anger that is more beneficial.

TEST ANXIETY

Many students face test anxiety at one time or another. Symptoms of test anxiety include: prior to exam, a fear of failing; tension; negative thinking; "brain fade" or "blanking out"; recalling information after the test is over; and so on. To reduce test anxiety, prepare and study ahead of time (try not to "cram" the night before), get plenty of rest, arrive early, eat something nutritious, and think positively.

Biologically, stress promotes hopelessness, despair, depression, helplessness, disappointment, exhaustion, worry, ailments, and as a result, self-medication is what many people resort to.

© ArtmannWitte/Shutterstock.com

STRESS MANAGEMENT STRATEGIES

Stress Management Strategy 1: Avoid Unnecessary Stress

Not all stress can be avoided, and it's not healthy to avoid a situation that needs to be addressed. You may be surprised, however, by the number of stressors in your life that you can eliminate. Learn how to say "no"; avoid people who stress you out; take control of your environment; avoid hot-button topics; cut down your to-do list.

Stress Management Strategy 2: Alter the Situation

If you can't avoid a stressful situation, try to alter it. Figure out what you can do to change things so the problem doesn't present itself in the future. Often, this involves changing the way you communicate and operate in your daily life: Express your feelings instead of bottling them up; be willing to compromise; be more assertive; manage your time better.

Stress Management Strategy 3: Adapt to the Stressor

If you can't change the stressor, change yourself. You can adapt to stressful situations and regain your sense of control by changing your expectations and attitude: Reframe problems; look at the big picture; adjust your standards; focus on the positive.

Stress Management Strategy 4: Accept the Things You Can't Change

Some sources of stress are unavoidable. You can't prevent or change stressors such as the death of a loved one, a serious illness, or a national recession. In such cases, the best way to cope with stress is to accept things as they are. Acceptance may be difficult, but in the long run, it's easier than railing against a situation you can't change: Don't try to control the uncontrollable; look for the upside; share your feelings; learn to forgive.

Stress Management Strategy 5: Make Time for Fun and Relaxation

Beyond a take-charge approach and a positive attitude, you can reduce stress in your life by nurturing yourself. If you regularly make time for fun and relaxation, you'll be in a better place to handle life's stressors when they inevitably come.

Stress Management Strategy 6: Adopt a Healthy Lifestyle

You can increase your resistance to stress by strengthening your physical health: Exercise regularly; eat a healthy diet; reduce caffeine and sugar; avoid alcohol, cigarettes, and drugs; get enough sleep; don't get so caught up in the hustle and bustle of life that you forget to take care of your own needs. Nurturing yourself is a necessity, not a luxury.

QUICK FIXES WHICH ARE NOT RECOMMENDED

Alcohol	Heavy drinking can lead to heart disease, liver disease, brain dysfunction, cancer and permanently disordered sleep.
Tobacco	Prolonged use impairs circulation & respiration and disturbs sleeping patterns; it increases the risk of a variety of cancers as well as the risk of cardiac disease.
Chocolate	Sugar may contribute to cavities, weight gain, & help induce diabetes in some people.
Sleeping Pills	Can cause lethargy and impaired performance during waking periods. May disturb sleeping patterns.
Coffee	Gradual tolerance develops, >3 cups a day may lead to irregular heart beat, headaches, muscle tension, irritability & insomnia.
Tranquilizers	When taken for more than three days, can cause lethargy, aggravate insomnia, and nightmares. May lead to drug dependence, fatigue, and feelings of depression.
Herbal Teas	Some, such as sassafras has been banned by U.S. Govt. as a cancer-causing agent. Others can be pleasant and soothe digestion.

TIME TIPS

Be ruthless with time and gracious with people.
Make a TO DO list and keep it in a prominent place.
Assign priorities to TO DO items and stick to priorities you set.
Know when enough is enough—don't try to be a perfectionist.
Ask the question: What could happen if I don't do this project?
Get an early start on things.
Handle hardest tasks at your best hours.
Do it now. Don't procrastinate on important tasks.
Avoid doing things yourself which should be assigned to subordinates.
Allow others to do a task their own way.
Learn to say NO gracefully but clearly.
Remember it takes two to make small talk.
In meetings, don't introduce extraneous information or comments.
Make all your phone calls at the same time each day.
Jot down points you want to make before telephoning.
Group your calls for greater efficiency.
Put a note on the phone: "Am I taking too long?"
Handle each piece of paper only once.

(*Continued*)

TIME TIPS (*Continued*)

When you read a letter or memo, jot notes to include in a reply. If a reply can be done by handwritten note, do it while you read.

Read incoming mail at the point when you plan to begin action on each piece requiring attention.

Don't overreact to crises and problems.

Keep your cool and delay responding when possible.

Be present and future oriented. Don't waste energy worrying about the past.

—Source of wisdom unknown

RISK

To laugh is to risk appearing the fool.

To weep is to risk appearing sentimental.

To reach out for another is to risk involvement.

To expose feelings is to risk exposing your true self.

To place your ideas, your dreams before the crowd is to risk their loss.

To love is to risk not being loved in return.

To live is to risk dying.

To hope is to risk despair.

To try is to risk failure.

But risks must be taken, because the greatest hazard
in life is to risk nothing. The person who risks
nothing, does nothing, has nothing and is nothing.
He may avoid suffering and sorrow, but he simply
cannot learn, feel, change, grow, love—live.
Chained by his certitudes, he is a slave, he has
forfeited freedom. Only a person who risks is free!

—Author Unknown

STRESS AND PERSONALITY TYPES

Type A personality is characterized by competitive, aggressive, and hostile attitudes and behavior. Research cardiologists working in San Francisco, Friedman and Rosenman, described these individuals as people who are always trying to achieve or acquire more and more things. These people put themselves under enormous pressures. Below are some of their common characteristics:

Competitive—Want to win at everything, even with children.
Hard-Driving—Push to limits that most people resist.

Unable to Relax—Even on vacation, they try to be productive.

Easily Angered—Very short fuses, & anger cuts all barriers.

Very Time Conscious—A watch is a necessity. Strict schedules.

Body language is also common with Type A Personality. A few exhibits:

Grimacing—Contorting their faces to express displeasure.
Tightening of Facial Muscles—Face, neck, and forehead.

Gesturing with a Clenched Fist—Clench and punch at points.

Using Explosive Speech—Change in vocal tone with loud bursts.

Hurrying the Pace—Try to speed along the pace.

Interrupting Others—Cutting people off before they are done.

TYPE A BEHAVIOR TEST

This scale, based on the one developed by Friedman and Rosenman, the higher number of yes responses will give you an estimate of your type A tendencies. Directions: Answer the following questions by indicating the response that most often applies to you.

YES	NO		Statement
____	____	1.	I always feel rushed.
____	____	2.	I find it hard to relax.
____	____	3.	I attempt to do more and more in less and less time.
____	____	4.	I often find myself doing more than one thing at a time.
____	____	5.	When someone takes too long to make their point, I finish the sentence for them.
____	____	6.	Waiting in line for anything drives me crazy.
____	____	7.	I am always on time or early.
____	____	8.	In a conversation, I often clench my fist and pound home important points.
____	____	9.	I often use explosive outbursts to accentuate key pts.
____	____	10.	I am competitive at everything.
____	____	11.	I tend to evaluate my success by translating things into numbers.
____	____	12.	Friends tell me I have more energy than most people.
____	____	13.	I always move, walk, and eat quickly.
____	____	14.	I bring work home often.
____	____	15.	I tend to get bored on vacation.
____	____	16.	I feel guilty when I am not being "productive."
____	____	17.	I tend to refocus other people's conversations around things that interest me.
____	____	18.	I hurry others along in their conversations.
____	____	19.	It is agonizing to be stuck behind someone driving too slowly.
____	____	20.	I find it intolerable to let others do something I can do faster.

Source: Stress Reduction Workbook.

Type A personalities have been identified as having two times greater risk for developing cardiovascular disease than Type B personalities. **Type B** people are more relaxed and easy-going, have high self-esteem, are centered, and not as competitive. These people have lower incidence of daily hassles, because they are not as easily frustrated.

Type C Personality—Type C individuals are just as highly stressed as Type A's but do not seem to be at higher risk for disease than Type B's. The keys to successful Type C performance seem to be commitment, confidence, and control. Type C people are highly committed to what they are doing, have a great deal of confidence in their ability to do their work, and are in constant control of their actions. In addition, they enjoy their work and maintain themselves in top physical condition to be able to meet the mental and physical demands of their work.

Many experts now believe that emotional stress is far more likely to trigger a heart attack than physical stress. People who are impatient and readily annoyed when they have to wait for someone or something—an employee, a traffic light, in a restaurant line—are especially vulnerable.

Primary stressors are the original stressor that triggers the stress response. Secondary stressors are our illogical thoughts about the primary stressor which keep the response alive long after the initial event has passed.

STRESS MANAGEMENT ALTERNATIVES

There are many physiological and psychological benefits of being fit. Regular exercise is essential for stress management. Exercise is a powerful antistress activity. Some people have an exercise high after a vigorous workout. (Endorphins are neuropeptides, produced in the brain and spinal cord that produce a feeling of well-being. Serotonin, dopamine, and norepinephrine are neurotransmitters related to mood that are antidepressants which increase energy and elevate mood. These neurotransmitters are released by the body as a byproduct of sustained exercise.) Numerous studies have shown that thirty minutes or more of moderate aerobic exercise reduces anxiety, feelings of helplessness, depression and hostility.

Exercise has also been shown to lower cholesterol level in blood, reducing the risk of atherosclerosis (deposits of cholesterol-laden blockages). In addition, exercise lowers the incidence of hypertension, (by putting the stress hormones released to work), and lessens the risk of cancer, stabilizes personality, increases self-esteem, reduces muscle tension very effectively, and can improve your sex life.

Laughter is one of the best medicines for stress reduction. You should take yourself lightly while you take your work seriously. It is physiologically impossible to be stressed, when you are laughing. Initially the processes of breathing, blood pumping, and muscle contraction are higher than when at rest, but after a good laugh, are below normal resting levels—resulting in the same sense of deep relaxation and contentment. Laughter is also a proven pain reliever. Norman Cousins, author of The Power of Positive Thinking, found that 10 minutes of laughter provided up to 2 hours of pain-free sleep. Humor can be used to reduce chronic degenerative diseases.

A good cry can also have a beneficial effect on stress reduction. Tears may help remove chemicals that build up during an emotionally stressful situation—thereby restoring the body's chemical balance. Support groups can be equally empowering in combating the effects of stress. Do not suppress a good cry! It is nature's stress management for sadness, grief, and disappointment.

Passive Relaxation Alternatives to Stress Management

Relaxation. To understand what relaxation is about, watch a dog or cat seek out a warm spot in the sun, have a good stretch and lie down. When we take the time to relax, our minds are clear, our muscles are without tension, and our breathing is free and easy.

Deep Breathing. Breathing slowly means it should take several seconds to fill your lungs with air. It is not unusual to take 10 seconds to inhale or exhale in breathing exercises. This is an excellent first choice to reduce stress.

Meditation. Most meditators are like all of us. Some are old, some are young, but not necessarily sitting on top of a hill for long periods of time. A few believe this will heighten your awareness. A few benefits include: decreased metabolic and oxygen consumption; alpha waves increase—as in a restful awake state; heart rate decreases; blood pressure remains unchanged but regular meditators have lower blood pressure generally; respiration decreases. Types of meditation are: Object or focal point; Word, Phrase, Mantra Meditation (think of one when inhaling, two when exhaling); Sound Meditation (music affects our emotions); Visualization (relaxing scenes, etc.); Autogenic Training (a form of self-hypnosis using imagery to relax and warm up our bodies); Biofeedback (learning by measuring temperature, muscle tension, perspiration and brain wave activity).

Active Relaxation Alternatives to Stress Management

Systemative Muscle Relaxation. Chronic muscle tension is a common by product of stress. Sometimes we don't realize how tense we are until we receive warning signs from our bodies. Stretching on a regular basis is a key. Suggested procedure:

1. Find a quiet place, minimize distractions, and lie on your back with your knees slightly bent, arms at your sides.
2. Point both toes—hold a few seconds, then relax (2 Reps)
3. Straighten both legs, contract your legs, then relax. (2 ×)
4. Tighten your stomach muscles, hold, then relax. (2 ×)
5. Contract your buttocks, hold a few seconds then relax. (2 ×)
6. Grasp your elbows with your hands and lift your arms over your head; tilt your head and arch your back—hold/relax.
7. Shrug your shoulders, hold a few seconds, then relax.
8. Clench your fists and curl arms up; hold, then relax.
9. Bend your head forward & hold, backward & hold, then sides.
10. Scrunch your face to make a funny face then relax.

Yoga and Static Stretching. Yoga involves an eightfold process:

1. Yama—rules and restraints for productive living in society, such as being truthful
2. Niyama—self-rules governing cleanliness and personal contentment
3. Asaana—physical exercises called postures
4. Pranayama—deep-breathing training
5. Pratihara—freeing the mind from the senses
6. Dharana—focused concentration on an object
7. Dhyana—meditation
8. Smadhi—cosmic meditation.

T'ai Chi Ch'uan. This is referred to a moving meditation, and teaches people to remain calm and centered in the forces of opposition. It emphasizes conserving energy, remaining balanced, and using forces, rather than fighting them. It basically teaches people how to use homeostasis in the face of stress.

Massage and Therapeutic Touch. Massage was created by the Chinese, and some believe that healing through physical touch is accomplished as we produce and transfer energy to each other. Types of massage include Swedish (or total body massage); Shiatsu (or acupressure massage); and Medical/Sports Massage.

WORKSHEET 7

NAME ______________________

The following is a list of stress inducing events, in the order of their Life Change Unit. Note all the items that apply to events you have experienced **during the last year.**

Life Event	Life Change Unit
1. Death of spouse	100
2. Divorce	73
3. Marital Separation	65
4. Jail Term	63
5. Death of a close family member	63
6. Personal injury or illness	53
7. Marriage	50
8. Being fired from work	47
9. Retirement	45
10. Change in health of family member	44
11. Pregnancy	40
12. Sexual difficulties	39
13. Addition of family member	39
14. Major change in financial state	38
15. Death of a close friend	37
16. Changing to a different line of work & responsibilities	36
17. Change in frequency of arguments with spouse	35
18. Children leaving home or Military Deployment	29
19. Outstanding personal achievement	28
20. Spouse begins or stops work	26
21. Starting or ending school	26
22. Change in living conditions	25
23. Revision of personal habits (dress, manners, associations)	24
24. Change in work hours, conditions	20
25. Change in residence	20
26. Change in school	20
27 Change in recreational or social activities	19
28. Change in sleeping habits	16
29. Change in eating habits	15
30. Vacation	13

You Received a Score of ____________

If your total is 0–150: Congratulations! At the moment, your stress level is low. Your chance of illness or accident related to your stress within two years is low.

If your total is 150–300: Take care of yourself now. You have borderline high stress. Your chance of accident or illness related to your stress within two years is moderate.

If your total is over 300: Warning: You have a high stress level. Your chance of accident or illness related to your stress during the next two years is great.

Source: Saddleback College (Based on the work of Thomas and Rahle)

PERSONAL STRESS MANAGEMENT TECHNIQUES

1. As a result of my score on the previous page, the following are four techniques that I have used to cope with those events which have recently occurred in my life.

   a.

   b.

   c.

   d.

2. What new techniques could you possibly rely on to help cope with stress in the future?

Glossary of Terms

Active/Passive Training refers to relaxation management techniques for reducing stress: Active could be muscle relaxation, yoga, T'ai Chi, or massage; Passive could be resting, deep breathing, or meditation.

Autogenic training is a stress management technique which is a form of self-suggestion where an individual is able to place him/herself in a state by repeating and concentrating on feelings of heaviness and warmth in the extremities.

Biofeedback is a process in which a person learns to reliably influence physiological responses of two kinds; either responses which are out of our control, and those which are easily regulated, but has broken down due to disease or trauma.

Catecholamine are stress hormones such as epinephrine and norepinephrine that are produced by the adrenal glands.

Distress is negative stress, and refers to unpleasant or harmful stress under which health and performance begin to deteriorate.

Eustress is positive stress which health and performance continue to improve, even as stress increases.

Fight or flight is a physiological response of the body to stress which prepares the individual to take action by stimulating the vital defense systems.

Meditation is used to gain control over one's attention, clearing the mind and blocking out the stressor(s) responsible for the increased tension.

Progressive relaxation involves contraction and relaxation of muscle groups throughout the body.

Psychosomatic results from a person who evidences bodily symptoms or bodily and mental symptoms as a result of mental conflict.

Stress is the general physical and psychological response of an individual to any real or perceived adverse stimulus, internal or external, that tends to disrupt the individual's homeostasis. Stress that is excessive or reacted to inappropriately, may cause disorders.

Stressor is the reaction of the organism to a stress-causing event.

Stress management is a group of skills for dealing with stresses imposed on an individual without suffering psychological distress and/or physical disorders.

Time management involves working efficiently with the lifestyle commitments we undertake. Allocating enough time which will contribute to our overall wiliness.

Type A personality is a behavior pattern characteristic of a hard-driving, overambitious, aggressive, chronically hostile, and overly competitive person.

Type B personality is a behavior pattern characteristic of a calm, casual, relaxed, and easy-going individual.

Type C personality is a behavior pattern of individuals who are just as highly stressed as the Type A but do not seem to be at higher risk for disease than the Type B.

Related Websites

Stress Management

- www.stresstips.com
- stress.about.com

Stress Management

- www.stresscontrol.com
- www.relaxintuit.com
- www.hypnosisaudio.com
- www.unl.edu
- www.futurehealth.org
- stress.org
- webond.com
- medicinenet.com/stress

STUDY QUESTIONS

NAME ____________________

1. How can stress be interpreted to be either a positive or a negative influence?

2. What is meant by the statement, "It is not the event, but how we view it," when dealing with stress?

3. Are there any stress symptoms or cues indicated in the chapter that *you* have been aware of in the past? Have any shown up repeatedly indicating a stress buildup?

4. What are the most common mistaken traditional assumptions that you have encountered? Were your legitimate rights utilized in any of these instances?

5. What are the different traits between personality types labeled A, B, and C?

Fitness for Life

KEY TERMS	
Exercise prescription	Sprain
Frequency	Strain
Heat cramps	Stress fracture
Heat exhaustion	Tendonitis
Heat stroke	Time
Intensity	Wellness
Shin splints	Workout

You feel healthy, have no major aches or pains and just kind of cruising along in your everyday adventure of school, job, grades, financial concerns and your future.

Then there is a news commentary, on television or in print, that all adults should take stock of their health and determine just how fit they are. But, you're a modern day student with an active yet busy agenda: school, a job or two, relationships, family, and possibly an appointment to see your medical practitioner in the near future, when you can afford it. So you go to your doctor and receive a complete physical examination, and now you wait for the results. Lo and behold, you are told to not exercise, continue your usual lifestyle of inactivity, poor nutritional intake, unidentified stress situations and to come back for a checkup when something really serious occurs.

Sound a little farfetched? Except for a short period of rest for a specific illness or injury, rarely would a physician tell a patient not to get physically active or exercise. Yet when you don't take the initiative to become active and pry yourself loose from the couch potato position, you are, in effect, THAT doctor writing that same prescription to yourself. It is important to realize that the farther into the future that we are separated from our ancestors, we fall victim to an apparently easier and less demanding lifestyle. Since their physically exacting life kept them healthy, and except for shorter lifespans due to outside sources of diseases and infections, their activity would offset a multitude of afflictions found in today's society. As technology moves ahead, the number of labor saving devices will continually erode further any required physical activity as part of our daily lives, in or out of school.

Recognize the fact that your recent lifestyle is represented in the results of the health related fitness areas: cardiovascular endurance, flexibility, body composition, muscle strength and endurance. You need to differentiate from the skill related areas of fitness, i.e. speed, reaction time, coordination, power, balance and agility. Since these relate to the acquisition of skill, they really are dependent on other factors covered later in this chapter.

HEALTH RELATED FITNESS AREA	LOWER FITNESS RATINGS MAY INCREASE THE RISK OF:
▪ Cardiovascular Endurance	□ Coronary heart disease □ Excessive body fat accumulation (lowered aerobic activity) □ Diabetes, Type II (adult onset)
▪ Flexibility	□ Low back injury or pain □ Decreased mobility in daily tasks □ Limited success in certain skill related activities, i.e. golf, tennis
▪ Body Composition	□ Coronary heart disease □ Diabetes, Type II (adult onset) □ Lowered self esteem □ Bone and/or joint problems □ Colon cancer
▪ Muscular strength and endurance	□ Lowered self esteem □ Bone and/or joint problems □ Osteoporosis □ Certain daily activities and sports

Table 8.1 Less than Desired Fitness Ratings and Possible Health Implication

The health related fitness test results are not to be considered a diagnostic tool for determining specific health problems. These are to be used as an educational resource and combined with knowledge acquired about the various health areas. The purpose is for you to become informed so that you can make intelligent and logical decisions about your health and fitness, now and in the future.

Obviously, when considering the implications of less than desired ratings of very poor, poor and possibly even fair in any specific area, judgments and decisions should be based on fact and not some myth. How will this rating interpretation have an impact on my future? (See Table 8.1.)

PHYSIOLOGY OF AGING

Aging, as defined by Dr. Roy Shepard, is "the diminished capacity to regulate the internal environment, resulting in a decreased probability of survival." Aging is an inevitable part of life for all species. Humans differ in their rates of aging based on many factors. We all know individuals in their 50s or 60s who are invalids and others who are in their 80s or 90s who are healthy, active and alert. Among factors which influence the aging process are genetics, disease, dietary habits and perhaps most important, physical activity/physical fitness level. It is estimated that by the year 2030, the number of Americas aged 65 and over will reach 70 million. The rate of decline is slower in the fit individual. Thus, the active person can remain self-sufficient for many years.

Remember, you are never too old or sedentary to begin a fitness program. Just because you have been on an exercise program for months or even years, don't misunderstand the need to consider some of the topics to follow. These suggestions apply to young and old, beginner to experienced, or neophyte to athlete. Its time to take stock of your present status and determine where do you want to be? What are you trying to accomplish? You need to define your goals. Some of you may just want to be healthy. Others may desire to look good, increase your self esteem, or to be visually pleasing with well toned muscles. Another group may be looking forward to developing certain fitness components to a higher level with possible competition lurking in the shadows. For those of you who are already exercising, why are you participating in that specific group of activities?

You've arrived at the beginning step of establishing a personal fitness program. Rather than just go aimlessly through the motions of exercise, without rhyme or reason, you should determine in what direction this program is headed. Identify your goal! Remember that the principle of specificity means that you get exactly what you train for. Now your goal may be to just be healthy. This is a large target to aim at. This will encompass a far reaching regimen of not only an exercise program, but, also incorporate sound nutritional practices, adequate stress management techniques to avoid mental and physical dysfunction and to not rely on any form of drugs to relieve anxiety. This chapter will deal more specifically with the fitness program via exercise. There will be many more health related benefits of the program if it is well rounded and not too narrow. The objective of being healthy can be broken down into smaller, easily identifiable and attainable goals.

Usually, after the holiday season starting with Thanksgiving and ending with New Years, there is a mad rush by many Americans to make new years' resolutions and to make up for their overindulgent behavior during this holiday period. Typically these people are not thinking clearly and make overly ambitious demands on their bodies to make up for lost time. Often this results in disillusionment or

possibly injury because the goal was too unrealistic to be accomplished in a short period of time. You don't want to set yourself up for failure and become an exercise or activity drop out, almost before you start. Their chance for success would be greater if their goal was not too grandiose or if they had allowed sufficient time for a more moderate approach to fitness. So, when determining fitness goals, divide them up into short term and long term.

Short term goals are easier to reach and therefore you will be more successful if it can be completed within a month. Once a goal is reached, another can be established and you keep on repeating this process. Eventually some long term goals may be met while others may still be off in the future.

An example of a short term goal may be to just become physically active. You have been living a very sedentary life for quite some time. To begin exercising in a program may be down the line. You are going to be more physically active than before by doing simple behavior changes. Walk more often, either before or after a meal. Walk instead of using a car for short trips. Park farther away at the mall, market or movie theatre. Take the stairs rather than the elevator. Small little steps until being physically active is a way of life. Specific fitness goals maybe difficult for the beginner to achieve in a short term basis. But an active lifestyle will become contagious, it will infect you and others around you, i.e. family, friends, or coworkers. This 'infection' will aid you in the support you give to yourself and the willingness of others to help you fulfill this new lifestyle change. It is important to let others (spouse, friends, family) know that you are trying to reach the goal of some type of daily physical activity. Another aspect for the beginner to consider is that small bouts of activity can be used. It doesn't have to be long and exhausting. If you are coming from a background of injuries or discouragement due to previous attempts to gain fitness, proceed with caution.

BENEFITS OF A PERSONAL FITNESS PROGRAM	
Decreases . . .	Increases . . .
Blood Pressure	Resting & maximum stroke volume
Resting heart rate	Maximum cardiac output
Total cholesterol	Maximum oxygen consumption
Body fat storage	HDL-cholesterol
Symptoms of depression	Aerobic work capacity

Table 8.2 Benefits of Cardiovascular Fitness

Good nutrition, regular physical activity, and stress management significantly contribute to achieving optimal health. By practicing these healthy lifestyle behaviors, excess weight is prevented, weight loss is sustained, and strength and endurance are achieved. The reward is invigorating, energizing, joyous health. It is a level of health that allows people to embrace each day and live their lives to the fullest—without disease, disability, or lost productivity. (Surgeon General)

Once you gain success with frequent, if not daily, physical activity, it is time to begin aiming for some more short term fitness goals. Depending on what type of specific goal you have in mind, the most far reaching fitness activity should involve some form of aerobics. Since the cardiovascular benefits of aerobic exercise will contribute to your overall general health, then these are just some of the small positive changes as a result. (See Table 8.2.)

Selecting the type of aerobic activity is essentially the one that you like and will do. It is possible that you may not have experienced the activity before and only have heard about it. By now you should realize that progressing with caution and not to go too fast is the best approach. Take into consideration your general health, exercise background (if any), and the goal selected. Generally speaking, the less energy demanding, the longer the time line to achieve a fitness goal, but the less chance for injury. It is important to listen to your body. Only you can differentiate pain from soreness, although at the beginning it may be difficult to tell. You must expect that any time you move from one fitness plateau to another, you will experience a certain degree of discomfort. The body is testing something new and it will take time for the body to adapt. (S.A.I.D. principle). The body's schedule for conditioning may take many months. With time and exposure to these little annoyances, you will be able to identify possible causes, i.e. overdoing the activity, not warming up, or not cooling down properly. A cause of making you unable to exercise frequently occurs with former athletes, who have let time march on and have 'been on the shelf for a long period of time'. The competitive juices begin to flow if a weekend picnic for the company employees is coming up or a league is forming and tryouts are scheduled next week. A key phrase used in the past and probably will be used in the future: Get in shape to play, don't play to get in shape!!

© Andresr/Shutterstock.com

The aerobics mentioned in Chapter 2 covers a wide range of activities, so if you try some activity and don't like it, venture out and try something else. Remember, by doing anything new it will take time to get accustomed to the routine. Progress slowly. A good routine to follow is by combining various forms of aerobics, particularly when experimenting to find something new to go with your favorite exercise. Don't depend on only one type of aerobics to bring about fitness results. If done too often and/or too hard, boredom from repetitious routines may result, and overuse injuries may occur. If this situation happens, then there will be an interruption to your workout routine and that is not what this is all about. As you move into a more advanced fitness status, another form of relief from the monotony of repetitious work is in the form of cross training.

Cross training in this regard deals with a more diverse exercise program. This would involve aerobics for cardiovascular endurance, pre- and post stretching routines for increased flexibility, weight training for muscular strength and endurance and possibly incorporating an activity or sport purely for fun or skill enhancement. Cross training tries to combine exercise activity at various intensities involving different fitness components in a regular weekly program. It may be a very specific program because the short term goal is very specific. Train for a 10 K run. Prepare for a triathlon in 3–4 months. Try to look good for a high school reunion by losing 15 pounds of fat. All would require a different approach because of background, fitness level and motivation.

Short term goal(s) and possibly a long term one have been determined. Various activities have been selected that you like and will benefit you as you reach your goal(s). Step three has been reached and that is commitment. How dedicated are you in achieving these goals? You should plan on a set time of day to exercise, with a specific task to be accomplished for just that period. It may be a distance in a specific time, or repetitions with weights at a certain poundage, or set number of minutes for each phase of today's program. (See Table 8.3.)

10 min.	Warmup . . . . . light aerobics—calisthenics, jump rope
10 min.	Stretching overall body
30 min.	Circuit training with weights
20 min.	Aerobic workout . . . steady running
5 min.	Cool down/stretching

Table 8.3 Example of Daily Workout on Time Basis

The best plan of action is to have a plan of action. A written plan. A contract with yourself indicating your goals, tentative timetable to follow, possible list of activities you will engage in, and who will support you. A specific contract signed by you and others who will uphold your decision and maybe even coerce you into completing the agreement. Studies have shown that a person with a written plan and specific details is more likely to follow through and meet their goals. By keeping records of what you do, evaluation of your program is easy to determine. After a short period of time, maybe a few weeks, see if your plan is working or not. Are goals being met already? Is it time for a new program with another time frame? Or are you feeling you're on the right track but the results haven't kicked in yet? Were the goals too unrealistic and just too hard to reach for your present fitness level? Reevaluate your position.

But before you take that step, check with your doctor, especially if you're over 40, or if you have any health problems, like hypertension, high cholesterol, diabetes, a family history of heart disease or a smoker. You will probably get their encouragement, however, if you ever have unusual pain that may persist or if in doubt, always seek medical advice.

Once you begin making progress with your new lifestyle, or just continued success with your ongoing program of fitness, don't keep it a secret. Share these positive results with family, friends, co-workers or neighbors. Your attitude of confidence and well being will show through and hopefully validate your decision and possibly motivate others to become more active and follow your example. Repeatedly state positive affirmations about your new habits and lifestyle like "I am healthier now that I walk (exercise) 5 days a week," or "I have renewed energy with my new activities." Say them to yourself frequently, even to assume that you have already reached your goal.

As part of your original contract or the follow up contracts, you may want to include, beyond personal satisfaction and well being, a clause regarding a reward for accomplishments. Try to make the reward something meaningful yet not overly expensive. Something that reinforces your new active lifestyle, maybe new exercise shoes or clothing. It could be a gift to yourself of a movie or a dinner out. Don't go into debt over this reward, because, hopefully there will be others and don't indulge yourself with something, i.e. fatty foods, vacation from any exercise, etc., that will sabotage the result of all your efforts. Don't be afraid of your success. Enjoy it, you've earned the attention.

After some noteworthy goal has been achieved, or you have been more active than ever before, take the time to reflect on what you have done. You put in the time and sweat so reap the rewards. Remember, there is no substitute for regular exercise, particularly if you are trying to reach new fitness levels and a healthier lifestyle.

10 TIPS FOR REACHING PHYSICAL ACTIVITY GOALS

Physical activity does not need to be strenuous to bring health benefits. Whether it is a structured exercise program or just part of your daily routine, all exercise adds up to better health. Below are some tips for reaching your physical activity goals.

1. If you have not been active for a long time, are overweight, have a high risk of coronary heart disease or some other long-term health problem, see your doctor for medical evaluation before beginning a physical activity program.
2. Don't overdo it. Perform low to moderate-level physical activities that get your heart rate up, especially at first. These aerobic activities (e.g., brisk walking, jumping rope, stair climbing, jogging, or dancing) build endurance and burn calories.
3. Slowly increase the duration and intensity of your exercise as you become fit. Over time, work up to 30 to 60 minutes of physical activity, at least five days a week. If you can't dedicate a full 30 minutes to exercise, break your physical activity into three 10-minute intervals.
4. Choose activities that are fun, not exhausting. Try using music to keep you motivated and entertained.
5. Add variety. Try not to rely too much on one activity. Find several that you enjoy. That way, exercise will never seem boring or routine.
6. Wear comfortable, properly fitted footwear and clothing that is appropriate for the weather and the kind of physical activity you choose.
7. Find a convenient time and a safe place to get active. Try to make it a habit, but be flexible. If you miss an opportunity, work physical activity into your day another way.
8. Try wearing a pedometer, which measures the distance you travel on foot. Set a long-term goal of 10,000 steps a day, or about five miles. Monitor your average number of steps each day and then add several hundred more steps a day each week until you reach your goal.
9. Share your physical activity time with others. Make a date with a family member, friend, or co-worker to walk or ride bikes. Be an active role model for your children.
10. Keep a record of your physical activities and reward yourself. Nothing motivates like success!

THE RIGHT EXERCISE PROGRAM FOR YOU STARTS HERE

Home. Wherever you work out, at home or at a fitness facility, the key criteria to use is whether you will exercise or not. Can you separate yourself from all the household chores that will be still waiting for you even after you finish? Or will the sight of some unfinished project haunt you and prevent you from enjoying the workout? You can go out door, for the expense of a good pair of walking/running shoes and comfortable clothes and benefit from some aerobic activity. You may want to invest a modest amount in some light weights or a garage sale special of barbells and assorted benches. Whatever you do, you must use the equipment. Possession is 9/10's of the law but it doesn't help you get fit.

Fitness Club. Working out at home is certainly cheaper without the monthly dues and associated costs of membership and current sales promotions. But can you stick with a program at home by yourself or do you need group enthusiasm and motivational music and regularly scheduled classes? You may have a wider variety of activity choices at a fitness center, but also look for crowds, and for professionally trained instructors who are interested in your progress and desires and not neglect you after the initial introduction. The availability of the fitness club for use at all hours regardless of the weather may be a bonus. Check over the equipment you may be using for the condition and at the time you would be there. Is it too crowded and can you work your program without too much waiting around? Do the class offerings you're interested in coincide with your timetable? Do you feel comfortable exercising in a coed environment? Would it cramp your style? Ask your friends for recommendations that meet your activity requirements.

Deciding where to exercise comes down to picking the place that offers you the greatest comfort, and the one that works best with your lifestyle.

ENVIRONMENTAL CONCERNS

There are certain situations where your normal exercise program may need to be altered in order to safely complete the activity. Any atmospheric conditions that limit the capacity of your respiratory system to function properly need to be addressed. If pollen count is high affecting allergies, hay fever reactions, smog, colds, or other respiratory involved disorders are compromising your workout then adjustments have to be made to minimize the effects on your health. It may involve exercising earlier in the day before the air borne pollutants increase, or change to an indoor activity at home or at a club.

Try to keep cool when the temperatures rise may be easier to accomplish by simply following some guidelines for exercising in **hot weather.**

- Hydration. Make sure that you provide yourself with fluids, either water or a sports drink, before and after you exercise and even during the activity. Your body will lose a considerable amount of fluid through heat dissipation and sweat.
- Exercise Intensity. Try to reduce or slow down the effort you put forth as hotter days begin to arrive and your body has not had a chance to gradually adapt. Rather than fighting through a workout on an unusually hot day, you may want to postpone the workout or switch to a cooler time.
- Temperature. When temperatures go above 85°F, or when humidity is that high or higher, tread cautiously with outdoor activity. Cancel for the day or shift to early morning or evening.
- Clothing. Wear the least amount of clothing possible to allow for the heat to leave the body. Cotton or some other suitable material, that will allow for the evaporation of moisture, should be the fabric of choice as long as it was loose fitting.
- Rest. Don't become addicted to a workout schedule, regardless of the environment. Listen to your body and respect its message. Recovery from the previous workout is always critical and with the high temperatures it becomes doubly important.

© Pressmaster/Shutterstock.com

The other weather extreme of exercising outdoors in the **cold weather** has its own unique circumstances. A basic concern is the loss of body heat or hypothermia. To counteract this phenomenon, the proper amount and type of clothing will diminish the effects of the cold. Again, some guidelines to follow.

- Temperature and Wind. Watch out for conditions when the wind chill factor drops below −20°F. Exposed skin to that kind of cold weather is not advisable.
- Clothing. Dress in layers that can trap air next to the skin but still allow sweat to pass through the material. Avoid cotton or tightly woven clothes that will absorb the moisture and cause a chill. Depending on the activity, try to keep the feet warm and dry with proper footwear, hands warm with mittens (fingers are able to move against each other for heat) and wearing some form of covering will aid in reducing the excessive amount of heat loss from the head.
- Inhaled Air. Wear some form of material over the mouth and nose to warm the incoming cold air. This will allow for a normal breathing pattern to continue during the activity and avoid gasping upon direct contact with the cold air. A scarf or mask could be used.

SPECIAL POPULATIONS

Now what if you became **pregnant** (relax men, but still pay attention) and find yourself in either of two fitness situations. First, if you have been inactive, don't go and jump on the exercise bandwagon or line up at the added food line (now eating for two) without consulting with your doctor about getting on a special pregnancy workout program. The doctor will need to evaluate your health status and to determine if there are any special precautions to take. Many fitness facilities may have specific programs for the pregnant beginner, but almost in any case, walking would be a good start as long as you have comfortable supportive shoes.

If you fall into the second category of already exercising and getting in shape to become pregnant, you have now arrived! Your workout concerns are a little different, since you should cut back from a high impact aerobics to low impact exercises, possibly every other day. Another activity to consider would be to add some form of water exercises to your regimen. Since water will provide the buoyancy to support the added weight and associated lack of balance, swimming and aquatics would provide relief for some of the pressure and stress that a pregnancy may bring.

According to the American Council on Exercise, there are many physical benefits, and emotional ones, too. For example, a good exercise program may help relieve some of the common problems associated with pregnancy, like excessive weight gain, swelling of your hands and feet, leg cramps, insomnia, fatigue and constipation.

Improving posture, reducing backaches, facilitating circulation, reducing pelvic and rectal pressure, and increasing energy levels are all physical benefits you can look forward to if you follow a well-designed exercise program while you're pregnant. And let's face it, you'll feel better knowing you're doing something good for yourself. Exercising while you're pregnant can give you more confidence and help with those negative feelings that often seem to go along with pregnancy, weight gain, and ideas about upcoming labor and delivery.

Since **aging** is inevitable and affects both men and women, it is wise to consider an active and exercising lifestyle as early in the birthday counting period as possible. But, here the direction will deal with those who have reached 'senior', 'mature' or re-tired (not tired) status. So when you reach that plateau and are looking for the 'fountain of youth', put on your exercise clothes, walk all over your neighborhood, gradually adding more time each day and then return home. Repeat this trip frequently, even venturing out a little farther, or even in a different direction. After many such 'adventures' and upon your return one day, you have realized that some delivery company had already dropped off your package of 'youth', since now you're feeling better and enjoying life more.

© James Steidl/Shutterstock.com

Like the pregnant women, begin emphasizing the low impact activities if you've been inactive for a long period of time. A good program would include an easy aerobic warmup followed by a stretching routine. As your fitness level and energy reserve improve, try to gradually add more variety to your program, choose the exercises that you like and will do. If possible, add some muscular resistance exercises to go along with some other weight bearing activities in aerobics. By applying resistance to the body, bone density and connective tissue integrity will be increased, possibly delaying the effects of osteoporosis. All exercise activity recommended is conditional and that there are no apparent health problems and your doctor agrees to the exercise program.

When looking for the ideal program for you to follow, it is wise to clear up many **misconceptions** regarding fitness, exercise and fat loss. Let the buyer beware!

FITNESS FACTS

MISCONCEPTIONS	FITNESS FACTS
▪ Sit ups will reduce fat from the stomach	Abdominal exercises will not trim fat, need to reduce calories, add aerobics
▪ "No pain, no gain"	If you experience pain in the body frequently may be a warning of something more serious
▪ Muscle will turn to fat	Cell structure is different, may have fat added to the area
▪ Walking is not as good as running	Walking is fine for the majority, less chance for injuries, just takes longer to achieve results
▪ Saunas and body wraps eliminate cellulite	Melting fat off the body is not possible; squeezing the body will force the body fluids to another part of the body. Cellulite is a commercial word for fat that dimples
▪ Have to be in shape to exercise	Any exercise program can be tailored to match your fitness level
▪ You don't have to drink water unless thirsty	When you feel thirsty, it is too late, become hydrated before, during and after activity
▪ Stretch before you begin your exercise	You need to avoid exercising cold, tight muscles with an easy aerobic warm up and increase your body temperature first
▪ Weight lifting will decrease your flexibility	By lifting properly and going through ROM on each exercise will offset the increased muscle mass

F.I.T.
FORMULA FOR FITNESS

	Cardiovascular Endurance	Body Composition*	Muscle Strength	Muscle Endurance	Flexibility Stretching
F	3 Days a Week	5–7 Days a Week	3 Days a Week	3 Days a Week	5–7 Days a Week
I	60-75% Max. HR	40–60% Max. HR	70% 1 RM	40% 1 RM	Pain Free Stretching
T	20 Minutes Minimum	More than 30 Minutes	30 Min	30 Min	10–60 Seconds

*Body Composition should also include Strength Training 3 Days a Week.

© Mikael Damkier/Shutterstock.com

PHYSICAL ACTIVITY RELATED INJURIES

Many minor nagging injuries can be treated at home without medical intervention, unless it doesn't respond to the treatment within a short number of days (time varies). Try to apply the RICE principle as soon as possible after the incident . . . strains of muscles, tendons and ligaments, or sprains, bruised or just inflammation of the joints.

R.I.C.E: The Best Treatment for Most Injuries

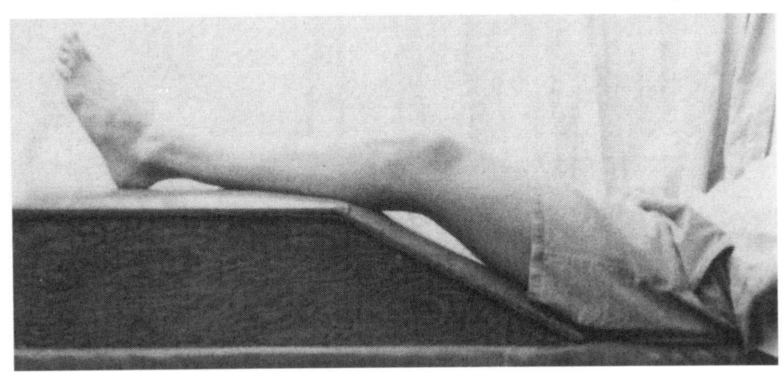

Figure 8.1 REST for approximately 48 hours after the injury to prevent reinjury and to allow healing.

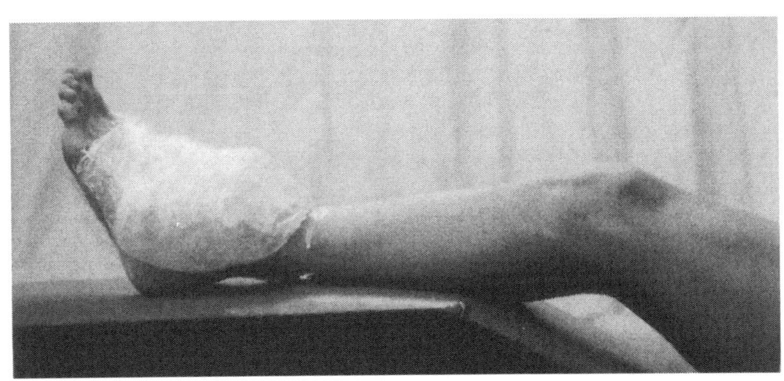

Figure 8.2 ICE packs will reduce bleeding from the torn blood vessels. Apply an ice pack (or cold water) to the injured area for 20 minutes every hour, over a 48 hour period if possible.

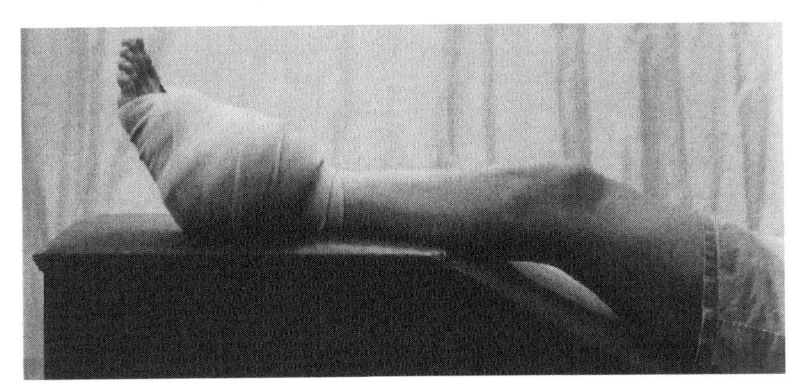

Figure 8.3 COMPRESSION should be used as with an ace bandage to contain the swelling. Firmly bandage the injured area, but don't bandage it so tightly that it will be uncomfortable, AND

Figure 8.1, 8.2, 8.3 ELEVATION is important, so that the injured area is raised allowing blood to flow towards the heart. This will reduce the pressure of fluid on the injured area.

WORKSHEET 8

NAME ______________________________

YOUR OVERALL FITNESS ASSESSMENT

	Fitness Category
LAB 1: Cardiovascular Endurance & Flexibility	
■ 12 Min. Run/Walk or 3 Min. Step Test	____________
■ Flexibility Test (Sit & Reach)	____________
LAB 2: Body Composition and Waist to Hip Ratio	
■ Body Fat Percentage (Skinfold Test)	____________
■ Waist to Hip Ratio (Measurement Tape)	____________
LAB 3: Muscle Endurance & Muscle Strength	
■ 1 Minute Curl Up Test	____________
■ 1 Minute Push up Test	____________
■ 1 RM Leg Press Test	____________
■ 1 RM Bench Press Test	____________
LAB 4: Skill-Related Fitness	
■ Agility Run or Fig. 8 Agility Test	____________
■ Dynamic Balance Test	____________
■ Power Test (Standing Long Jump)	____________
LAB 5: Aquatic Ability (5=Excellent, 4=Good, 3=Average, 2=Below Average, 1=poor)	
■ Front Freestyle	____________
■ Backstroke	____________
■ Breaststroke	____________
■ Elementary Backstroke	____________
■ Side Stroke	____________
■ Float	____________

DESIGN YOUR EXERCISE PROGRAM

1. Do you like to exercise by yourself or with others? ________________
2. How much time per day can you devote to exercise? ________________
3. Can you exercise during your school or work day? ________________
4. Do you start exercise programs but don't stick to them? ________________
5. Would an exercise program benefit your job? ________________
6. Do you prefer to exercise at home, gym, or school? ________________
7. Do you want to improve your health and fitness level? ________________
8. What lab or component of fitness concerns you most? ________________
9. Are you wiling to commit to a lifetime of exercise? ________________
10. Do you know the F.I.T. for each fitness component? ________________

PROGRAM PLAN TO IMPROVE AND ACHIEVE LIFETIME FITNESS

Activity	Sun.	Mon.	Tue.	Wed.	Thu.	Fri.	Sat.	Minutes
Walk		X		X			X	30 mins.

Critiqued By: ________________________________

Suggestions: ________________________________

Glossary of Terms

Exercise prescription is a recommendation for a course of exercise to meet desirable individual objectives for fitness. Includes activity types; duration, intensity, and frequency of exercise.

Frequency is how often a person repeats a complete exercise session (e.g. 3 times per week). Frequency, along with duration and intensity affect the effectiveness of exercise.

Heat cramps is muscle twitching or painful cramping, usually following heavy exercise with profuse sweating. The legs, arms and abdominal muscles are the most often affected.

Heat exhaustion is caused by dehydration (and sometimes salt loss). Symptoms include a dry mouth, excessive thirst, loss of coordination, dizziness, headache, paleness, shakiness and cool and clammy skin.

Heat stroke is a life-threatening illness when the body's temperature-regulating mechanisms fail. Body temperature may rise over 104 degrees F, skin appears red, dry and warm to the touch. The victim has chills, sometimes nausea and dizziness, and may be confused or irrational. Seizures and comas may follow unless temperature is brought down to 102 degrees within an hour.

Intensity is the rate of performing work; power. A function of energy output per unit of time. Intensity, along with duration and frequency, affect the effectiveness of exercise.

Kinesiology is the study of the principles of mechanics and anatomy in relation to human movement.

Shin splints is a pain in the front of the lower leg from inflammation of muscle and tendon tissue caused by overuse.

Sprain is stretching or tearing of ligaments. Severity ratings of sprains are: first-degree, stretching of the ligament; second-degree, partial tearing; third-degree, complete tears.

Strain is a stretching or tearing of a musculotendinous unit. Degrees of severity include: first-degree, stretching of the unit; second-degree, partial tearing of the unit; and third-degree, complete disruption of the unit.

Stress fracture is a partial or complete fracture of a bone because of the remodeling process' inability to keep up with the effects of continual, rhythmic, nonviolent stresses on the bone.

Tendonitis is inflammation of a tendon.

Time (duration) is the time spent in a single exercise session. Duration, along with frequency and intensity, are factors affecting the effectiveness of exercise.

Wellness is a state of health more positive than the mere absence of disease; wellness programs emphasize self-responsibility for a lifestyle process that realizes the individual's highest physical, mental and spiritual well-being.

Workout is a complete exercise session, ideally consisting of warm-up, intense aerobic and/or strength exercises, and cool-down.

Related Websites

Physical Activity and Health
www.cdc.gov/nccdphp/

Life Fitness
www.lifefitness.com

Fit Life
www.fitlife.com
fitness.com

AMA Health Insight
www.ama-assn.org/insight

Life Matters
www.lifematters.com
soplus.com

Study Questions

Name ______________________________

1. What is meant by the statement, ". . . your goals will help determine the type of activities you select to meet those goals"?

2. What are the criteria to consider when you begin planning a fitness workout program?

3. Who are the "special populations" that need to take a careful approach to physical exercise?

4. What specific environmental concerns do *you* come in contact with in your physical activity program? What alterations could you take to minimize the overall effects on your fitness?

Supplemental Definitions

Acclimation is a program undertaken to induce acclimatization to new environmental conditions such as changes in temperature/altitude.

Acute is a term for sudden, short-term, sharp or severe.

Adaptation are adjustments of the body (or mind) to achieve a greater degree of fitness to its environment.

Anemia is a subnormal number of hemoglobin content of red blood cells which is caused when blood loss exceeds blood production. Symptoms may include fatigue, pale complexion, light headedness, palpitations and loss of appetite.

Arthritis is inflammation of the joints which causes pain, stiffness and limitation of motion.

Atrophy is reduction in size, or wasting away, of a body part, organ, tissue or cell.

Basal metabolic rate is the minimum energy required to maintain the body's life functions at rest. Usually expressed in calories per hour per square meter of body surface.

Calisthenics is a system of exercise movements, without equipment, for the building of strength, flexibility and physical grace. The Greeks formed the word from "kalos" (beautiful) and "sthenos" (strength).

Carbon dioxide is a colorless, odorless gas that is formed in the tissues by the oxidation of carbon, and is eliminated by the lungs. Its presence in the lungs stimulates breathing.

Chronic is continuing over time.

Conditioning is long-term physical training.

Contraindication is any condition which indicates that a particular course of action (or exercise) would be inadvisable.

Dehydration is a condition resulting from the excessive loss of body water.

Detraining is the process of losing the benefits of training by returning to a sedentary lifestyle.

Energy is the capacity to produce work.

Exercise is physical exertion of sufficient intensity, duration, and frequency to achieve or maintain fitness, or other health or athletic, objectives.

Fatigue is the loss of energy to continue a given level of physical performance.

Heart attack is an acute episode of any kind of heart disease.

Homeostasis is the tendency of the body to maintain its internal systems in balance.

Hormone is a chemical, secreted into the bloodstream, that specifically regulates the function of a certain organ of the body. Usually, but not always, secreted by an endocrine gland.

Hyperthermia is body temperature exceeding normal.

Hypothermia is body temperature below normal. Usually due to cold temperatures, especially after exhausting ready energy supplies.

Infarction is death of a section of tissue from the obstruction of blood flow (ischemia) to the area.

Inflammation is the body's local response to injury. Acute inflammation is characterized by pain, with heat, redness, swelling and loss of function. Uncontrolled swelling may cause further damage to tissues at the injury site.

Ischemia is an inadequate blood flow to a body part, caused by constriction or obstruction of a blood vessel.

Kilocalorie (kcal) is a measure of the heat required to raise the temperature of one kilogram of water one degree Celsius. A large Calorie, used in diet and metabolism measures, that equals 1,000 small calories.

Medical referral is recommending a person see a qualified medical professional to review their health status and determine whether medical treatment is needed or whether a particular course of exercise and/or diet change is safe.

Met is a measure of energy output equal to the basal metabolic rate of a person at rest.

Osteoarthritis is a non-inflammatory joint disease of older persons. The cartilage in the joint wears down, and there is bone growth at the edges of the joints. Results in pain and stiffness, especially after prolonged exercise.

Overuse is excessive repeated exertion or shock which results in injuries such as stress fractures of bones or inflammation of muscles and tendons.

Ph is a measure of acidity, relating to the hydrogen ion (H+) concentration. A pH of 7.0 is neutral; acidity increases with lower numbers, and alkalinity increases with higher numbers. Body fluids have a pH of about 7.3.

Physical conditioning is a program of regular, sustained exercise to increase or maintain levels of strength, flexibility, aerobic capacity and body composition consistent with health, fitness or athletic objectives.

Physical fitness is the physiological contribution to wellness through exercise and nutrition behaviors that maintain high aerobic capacity, balanced body composition and adequate strength and flexibility to minimize the risk of chronic health problems and to enhance the enjoyment of life.

Proprioceptors are self-sensors (nerve terminals) that give messages to the nervous system about movements and position of the body.

Rehabilitation is a program to restore physical and psychological independence to persons disabled by illness or injury in the shortest period of time.

Steady state is the physiological state, during submaximal exercise, where oxygen uptake and heart rate level off, energy demands and energy production are balanced, and the body can maintain the level of exertion for an extended period of time.

Strain is a stretching or tearing of a musculotendinous unit. Degrees of severity include: first-degree, stretching of the unit; second-degree, partial tearing of the unit; and third-degree, complete disruption of the unit.

Stress fracture is a partial or complete fracture of a bone because of the remodeling process' inability to keep up with the effects of continual, rhythmic, nonviolent stresses on the bone.

Submaximal is less than maximum. Submaximal exercise requires less than one's maximum oxygen uptake, heart rate or anaerobic power. Usually refers to intensity of the exercise, but may be used to refer to duration.

Tachycardia is an excessively rapid heart rate. Usually describes a pulse or more than 100 beats per minute, at rest.

Tendinitis is inflammation of a tendon.

Testing protocol is a specific plan for the conducting of a testing situation; usually following an accepted standard.

Training is subjecting the body to repeated stresses with interspersed recovery periods to elicit growth in its capacity to handle such stresses.

Twitch is a brief muscle contraction caused by a single volley of motor neuron impulses.

Valsalva maneuver is a strong exhaling effort against a closed glottis, which builds pressure in the chest cavity that interferes with the return of blood to the heart. May deprive the brain of blood and causing fainting.

Vasoconstriction is the narrowing of a blood vessel to decrease blood flow to a body part.

Vasodilation is the enlarging of a blood vessel to increase blood flow to a body part.

Vital capacity is maximal breathing capacity; the amount of air that can be expired after a maximum inspiration; the maximum total volume of the lungs, less the residual volume.

Vital signs are the measurable signs or essential bodily functions, such as respiration Rate, heart rate, temperature, blood pressure, etc.

References

American College of Sports Medicine: *ACSM Fitness Book,* 2nd ed. Champaign: Human Kinetics, 1998.

American College of Sports Medicine: *Guidelines For Exercise Testing and Prescription,* 4th ed. Philadelphia: Lea & Febiger, 1991.

American Council on Exercise. *Personal Trainer Manual.* San Diego: American Council on Exercise Publishers, 1991.

Bailey, Covert. *Total Body Power.* New York: St Martin's Press., 1997.

Borg, G.V. "Psychological Basis of Perceived Exertion". *Medicine and Science in Sports and Exercise,* 14. 377–381

Branner, Toni Tickel. *The Safe Exercise Handbook.* Dubuque: Kendall/Hunt Publishing Co., 1989.

Clark, Nancy. *Sports Nutrition Guidebook: Eating to Fuel Your Active Lifestyle.* Champaign: Leisure Press, 1990.

Cooper, Kenneth H., M.D. *The Aerobics Program for Total Well-Being.* New York: M. Evans & Co., 1982.

Corbin, Charles B. and Ruth Lindsey. *Concepts of Physical Fitness.* 9th ed. Dubuque: Brown & Benchmark Publishers (A Times Mirror Company), 1997.

Fahey, Thomas D., Paul M. Insel, and Walton T. Roth. *Fit and Well,* 3rd ed. Mountain View: Mayfield Publishing Company, 1999.

Greenberg, Jerrold S. and George B. Dintiman. *Wellness: Creating a Life of Health and Fitness.* Boston: Allyn & Bacon, 1997.

Greenberg, Jerrold S., George B. Dintiman and Barbee Myers Oakes. *Physical Fitness and Wellness.* Boston: Allyn & Bacon, 1995.

Hockey, Robert V., Ed.D. *Physical Fitness: The Pathway to Healthful Living.* 8th ed. St. Louis: Mosby Publishers, 1996.

Hoeger, Werner W.K. and Sharon A. Hoeger. *Lifetime Physical Fitness & Wellness: A Personalized Program,* 4th ed. Englewood: Morton Publishing Co., 1995.

Institute of Aerobics Research. *The Advanced Physical Fitness Specialist Manual.* Dallas: IAR, 1991.

Jackson, Andrew S. P.E.D. and Robert M. Ross, M.D. *Understanding Exercise for Health and Fitness,* 3rd ed. Dubuque: Kendall/Hunt Publishing Co., 1997.

Jenkins, F. Compton. *Dynamics of Fitness and Health,* 7th ed. Dubuque: Kendall/Hunt Publishing Co., 1997.

Kosich, Daniel. Ph.D. *Get Real: A Personal Guide to Real-Life Weight Management.* San Diego: International Association of Fitness Professionals Publishers, 1995.

Melograno, Vincent and James Klinzing. *An Orientation to Total Fitness.* 5th ed. Dubuque: Kendall/Hunt Publishing Co., 1992.

Prentice, Wm. E. Ph.D. *Get Fit Stay Fit.* St. Louis: Mosby-Year Book, Inc., 1996.

Sharkey, Brian J. Ph.D. *Fitness and Health.* 4th ed. Champaign: Human Kinetics, 1997.

Tally, Jackie. *The Fitness Workbook.* 3rd ed. Dubuque: Kendall/Hunt Publishing Co., 1995.

Williams, Melvin H. *Lifetime Fitness and Weliness,* 3rd ed. Dubuque: WCB Brown & Benchmark Publishers, 1993.

Wuest, Deborah A. and Charles A. Bucher. *Foundations of Physical Education and Sport,* 13th ed. Dubuque: WCB McGraw-Hill, 1999.

Index

T